The Untended Soul
The Path to Light...and a Lighter Way of Being

By Stacey Morris

Book design by Robert McLearren

Dedication

For all who have struggled, may you realize the incomparable worth of your soul...

I Asked For Strength...
And Life Gave Me Difficulties
To Make Me Strong

I Asked For Wisdom...
And Life Gave Me Problems to Solve

I Asked For Prosperity...
And Life Gave Me Brain and Brawn to Work

I Asked For Courage...
And Life Gave Me Danger to Overcome

I Asked For Love...
And Life Gave Me Troubled People to Help

I Asked For Favors...
And Life Gave Me Opportunities

I Received Nothing I Thought I Wanted

I Received Everything I Asked For
 - Unknown Author

I began this decade-long series of essays and blog posts in 2009, which was the beginning of a cataclysmic life shift that included a 180-pound weight loss. In spite of this fact, this book is not a how-to for losing weight. Think of it more as a primer for tending to that intangible essence we all have and is all to often ignored. If, like me, you were encouraged from an early age to focus on your body because it wasn't quite right, then in all likelihood, that cloistered-away, incorporeal part of you has almost certainly been neglected. And it's not your fault. We have long lived in an appearance-focused culture and it's only become more obsessive where perfection and 'shoulds' are concerned.

I mention my weight transformation throughout the book because it's part of my story. Dropping a significant amount of weight is understandably fascinating given the culture we're living in, but I want to make clear that this book is about nurturing your inner-self. Weight-loss may or may not be an eventual side-effect. I began working on my soul and tending to its neglect nearly 33 years ago at age 21 following a painful childhood that included liberal amounts of scrutiny and criticism, very little nurturing, and lots of weight fluctuation thanks to the toxic pastime known as dieting.

I was worn out by the process of losing and regaining weight and by the time I'd reached the tender age of 21, knew that the quest for the acceptable body held no meaning whatsoever in the scheme of life. So, I enlisted the help of the best and most esteemed psychotherapist in our little upstate New York city. Dr. Mintz charged a pretty good buck for her services, and I didn't remain under her guidance for long because of financial restraints, but she opened the door to self-inquiry for me and I have never looked back. From there it was a steady stream of self-help books, Overeaters Anonymous meetings, past life regressions, group therapy, and even a month-long stay in a food-addiction rehab. I sought help anywhere I could find it. I was willing and ready to dig through the debris and to feel the sting of the wounds I tried so hard to ignore with trance-eating.

People see my weight-loss success story in magazines, on YouTube and various forms of social media. They're understandably inspired by it and I adore the idea of giving others hope…but I want to be clear on providing the full picture. The weight being shed and kept off this time around was preceded by a decades-long vision quest involving the proper care and feeding of my soul. Evolution has no timetable so I gave up imposing one on myself. I stopped being so concerned about my external qualities and what the world thought of me. Part of healing for me included rebel-eating and weight-gain without judgment. I would not be where I am today had I not allowed myself unmitigated freedom with food and the dignity of self-acceptance at any size.

Much of my soul-tending has been done solitude; getting right with myself had to include significant amounts of quiet reflection as well as an unhurried gestation period for new and healthier belief systems to blossom from papery saplings into solid, multi-branched oak trees. That's not to say it's entirely a solo expedition: I couldn't have done this without the support of fellow-sufferers, friends, family, therapists, and mentors. Through trial and error, I learned the balance between self-reliance and the need to lean on others.

There's no doubt my before and after pictures are inspiring, even soul-stirring, but please don't take them as some sort of finish line. The journey of evolution never ends. Contrary to what books and magazines endlessly imply, weight-loss does not mean and never has meant the cessation of problems: internal AND external. Remember, these essays span a decade. Sometimes, I refer to my weight as 165, sometimes it's 175. At one point, it leapt to a high of 214 pounds following a period of mourning and deep emotional anguish. That's life. I'm neither a robot or fitness model. If I'm to be a poster-girl for anything it's honesty. Life is uneven. Some days I struggle with weight, wanting food more than I'd like to, with comparing myself to others, and with not feeling good about myself. The difference is now, I have perspective, viable tools, and a wisdom that come with middle age. I use all of it to my advantage and I thankfully have a deep-rooted desire to not return to a life of unconscious denial.

My three previous works are cookbooks on healthy eating. Like the cookbooks, this collection of essays is intended to be a blueprint for you to take on your journey as an illustration that

5

freedom from bondage is possible. The turnaround I've done with my body was preceded by transfiguring my self-esteem from shaky to strong. I hope that in sharing these stories from my life you realize that the same can happen for you. Happiness and freedom aren't just a pipe dream…they are attainable and within reach.

Stacey Morris
August 11, 2018

What Others Are Saying:

Most of us think happiness is something we find 'out there'. Truth is, the keys are within our selves. But it takes time, patience and trust to mine those inner gems. Stacey Morris has done that work and continues to do so. In her quest to find her happiness she provides guideposts for all of us. Her words encourage us to be courageous when the tumult of the world threatens to push us backwards. Her journey helps show us that we can all find our inner beauty and unlock our strengths so we can be our best, and that it's helping others be their, that in the end, leads us to happiness. I am always uplifted after spending time with Stacey because she is so generous with her light. It never fails to help me on my path. I have no doubt that her latest book will help you as well.

- Benita Zahn, DPS
Anchor/Reporter
WNYT, NBC-affiliate, Albany, N.Y.

A lot of people reach out to me for help in getting their health back on track, but many either aren't serious about the commitment or just aren't ready to leave their comfort zone. Stacey was ready... I first met her when she started doing my DDP Yoga program in 2009. My close friend Terri Lange, known as the Godmother of DDPY (because she was my first weight-loss success story) called me to let me know she had met Stacey on our Team DDPYOGA community site. Terri told me Stacey had been doing the program for the past 3 months and had already lost 30 pounds and she thought I'd like to call her. Terri was right, I called Stacey as soon as we hung up.

During our first conversation, I jumped right in with what I believed she needed to do next if she wanted my help. Stacey agreed to almost everything but she was very resistant to the idea of taking the before pictures. She explains the full story of what happened in her chapter **"Put Your Hands in the Air Where I Can See 'Em and Drop the Denial"** Terri Lange and decided to co-mentor Stacey with advice on nutrition and the DDPY workouts. Stacey proved over and over that she was willing to listen, take advice, and put it to use in a way that worked for her. When Stacey gave up gluten and cow dairy at my suggestion, I mean, insistence) her weight really began to peel off. She was dedicated to the DDPYOGA workouts and kept challenging herself in different ways, like walking a marathon in New York City about 9 months into her journey and 100 pounds down. I loved hearing the enthusiasm in her voice as she revealed the milestones along her journey: she could wear jeans again, wear colorful clothing, take an airplane flight without needing a seatbelt extension, and go to concerts because she could fit in the seats again! Basically, all the work she did gave Stacey a whole new life.

A great ending to a Cinderella story, right? Well not quite. Life's not a Disney movie – there are harsh realities sometimes. Stacey has always been up front about being an emotional eater who regained 100 pounds – TWICE. Because of this, Stacey knew she'd have to come up with strategies for coping with life's curve balls….without turning to food. I've coached thousands of people over the years and those with weight issues who don't learn how to handle problems without food inevitably gain some or all of their weight back. But that doesn't have to be a given.

Stacey is living proof that the odds don't have to beat you. I've watched her handle upheaval, stress, grieving, and definitely, the triumphs she has achieved. Ten years later, the guidance Terri and I gave her turned from advice to a healthy way of living that has become Stacey's new normal. A big part of keeping herself healthy means taking care of the whole picture. Her other books were about cooking, but this one really has my attention because it's about coping. When Stacey lost 180 pounds in 18 months most people assumed that she had the surgery…Wrong! The truth was she did it through hard work. She trained hard, she focused on eating real food and more importantly, she put the work in on her soul.

If you're frustrated by yo-yo dieting, regaining weight, or just plain not feeling great about yourself, this book is for you. "The Untended Soul" will help build your self-esteem, destroy your destructive habits, and help you understand what's holding you back. It's got practical tools for making a better life from someone who's been there. As her mentor, I'm glad I was able to help Stacey reclaim her life and freedom, and even more thrilled that she continues to give others hope that anything is possible! Stacey is truly OWNING it, and you can too!

- Diamond Dallas Page (DDP)
  Creator & CEO of DDPY

Stacey has gone where many choose not to go, and has emerged a renewed and wiser person. Her weight-loss transformation is one of inspiration and struggle, but it's the way Stacey has bravely faced her past wounds and emotional demons that is most inspiring to me. As a nutritionist, I know all to well the quick fixes that are peddled in the worlds of weight-loss and wellness. Americans with emotional eating issues who are hooked into the instant gratification response are particularly vulnerable to this, and Stacey spent a considerable amount of time and energy wading through the empty promises and rising from the ashes. In the end, it was her inner-journey that saved her from a lifetime of denial and obesity. Not always an easy path, but Stacey rose above all self-doubt and negative-talk to finally reach optimal health of body and mind.

It has been remarkable to work with Stacey and watch her transformation from the inside out. She has achieved LONGTERM success by living an honest, emotionally accountable life...in addition to good nutrition. There's really an extra set of rules for the emotional eater: good nutrition and exercise aren't enough and that's precisely why Stacey struggled for most of her life. Thankfully, she has figured it out and shares it with readers to apply their own lives in a way that works for them.

Whether your desire is to get rid of excess weight or simply feel better about who you are, Stacey's compassionate honesty is a much needed tonic in an arena famous for manipulation and deception. Think of "The Untended Soul" as an empathetic wake-up call and a beginning step in giving you the inspiration and confidence you need to begin your own journey and eventually, reach your goals.

Nancy Guberti
Certified Holistic Nutritionist
Functional Medicine Specialist

Stacey began as my student ten years ago and has now become MY teacher by sharing her weight loss journey and delicious, healthy-eating recipes in her first books. I am so grateful that she continues to choose to help others find their own healthy journeys. Stacey continues to pay it forward as I have done with her, and Dallas Page did for me! And now, with her latest book, she shares her soul, inner-thoughts, triumphs, and tears. Through revealing herself, Stacey reveals that losing weight is NOT just about dieting but rather, more about nourishing your soul and spirit. She has learned how to eat to live rather than living to eat. Though a long, honest, and sometimes frustrating journey, Stacey has freed herself, and I hope this book will encourage others to free themselves!

-      Terri Lange, AKA The Godmother of DDPYOGA

"Stacey - I've been working on the issue of obesity for nearly 40 years, and I want to say that your take on the subject via your Huff Post blog is the most thoughtful, useful, insightful, and powerful comment I have ever seen."

-      Art Ulene, M.D.

Former "Family Doctor" for the Today Show

Table of Contents

~ Feelings ~

Healing the Hurt Heart

This isn't my term; it's from a reader of my blog who sent me a beautiful letter today. She's frustrated with herself because she hasn't 'gotten it' yet, and as such is flailing about in the sticky web known as emotional eating, weight gain, and the ensuing self-loathing. And the exasperated letter-writer knows that for many years, I was in a place that seemed like a million miles away from getting it.' I'm not entirely sure "getting it" is proper terminology anyway, for it implies arriving at a destination… journey over. I don't want to put that much pressure or adulation on myself. The only thing I'm an expert in is my mistakes and learning from them. It's no easy task attempting to define an issue that's too vast and nebulous to define. But here's what I know, based on a quick outline of my life:

Childhood – The unsuspecting, happy, curious-about-the-world kid has no idea when she steps onto the school bus that her largeness is a crime against humanity punishable by emotional torture to be administered by secretly (but profoundly) insecure and unhappy boys and girls for the remainder of her years in the public school system. Irony of ironies: In the beginning, I wasn't really 'fat.' I was larger and taller than most of the kids, but as childhood pictures have proven, the 'f' word didn't apply to me in my early years.

Adolescence – After years of hearing the verbal reinforcements that I was fat (and ugly and stupid) I began to become that.

Try focusing on math and social studies while putting your back into the construction and maintenance of a massive front that tells the world, 'Oh everything's just fine..." Pain...What's that?' But inside I was hurting. Significantly. And what do fat, abhorrent slobs do? They eat like pigs. May as well enjoy some food if people have already decided I'm fat. An added bonus: it dulled the pain and made me feel better.

20's – Teen years of crash dieting and bingeing, sneaking food, and despising myself with a passion leave me burnt out and hopeless. Life intervenes with a hypnosis tape for weight loss given to me as a Christmas gift. I fall asleep to it every night for a year and drop 100 pounds. I'm delighted with the transformation because now it means I'm OK. At last, I'm a valid human being worthy of respect and admiration...and maybe a few bushels of rose petals showered before me wherever I walk. Ah, but there's a snag. I haven't changed on the inside. I still see myself as the flawed and unlikable creature that was singled out on the school bus; the daughter my mother was ashamed of; the one who weighed more than most football players. And wait a minute...why are people being nice to me now? I'm the same person...and I'm not sure I like all these guys suddenly leering in my direction. See 'ya!

30's – After living through two100-pound weight losses and subsequent regains, I've had enough. Doesn't life have more in mind for me than loving food more than everyone says I should accompanied by the emotional burden of weighing more than everyone says I should? And I'm up to my eyeballs in the psychological fatigue of hating myself, courtesy of school bullies and a society that demands I look a certain way in order to be accepted. Haven't millions of years of intelligent life evolving on planet earth led us further than this? I decide there's got to be more to the human experience, and give up both dieting and the desire for other people's approval for-EVER. I create a new syllabus for my life. A course outline that includes radical self-acceptance, which begins with getting to know who the heck I am without the labels and stereotypes put in place by the fat-phobic culture that's uniquely American. And I realize that

part of the flowering journey into acceptance includes eating…
without shame. The only thing that's off-limits and not allowed
is self-recrimination. It feels unsafe and a little awkward, but I
take the leap of eating in public. Even in front of my mother.
Even foods that I 'shouldn't' be eating. And about those
knuckle-draggers who thought it was appropriate to verbalize
their disapproval of my size during this era…I'm at long last
ready to summon my outrage and fury where it needs to be sent
and have no trouble spinning around on my heel to confront the
jeering hecklers. I may not reverse their opinion, but they get
the message in no uncertain terms that this is one fat chick they
can't dump on. And bonus: I had no idea how off-the-charts
satisfying it is to confront and command respect, and in some
cases, watch the fat-haters scatter like rats rather than look me
in the eye.

40's – I continue to master self-acceptance with flying colors.
Yes, it's easier said than done, but here's a hint to get you started:
You decide you're tired of carrying the load around and put it
down. And by load I don't mean what's on your hips or stomach.
Emotional baggage and decimation to your self-worth is far
more burdensome to drag around on a daily basis. Perhaps
it was a simple matter of battle fatigue for me and realizing I
have a choice in how I view myself and how I allow others to
treat me. I'm the first to admit how scary and overwhelming it
might sound…especially if you've been living with the dynamic
for years and years. Those around you have come to expect
complacency, people-pleasing, and door-mat-status from you. I
know – I lived this way. Until one day I couldn't. Just know, that
as a former door-mat and recovering people pleaser…freedom
is possible, but everyone has their own timetable. Another
hallmark of my 40's: I continue to enjoy food fully, in a more
healthy way than in my teens and 20's. I no longer eat in hiding,
but with friends and family in ways that are celebratory. I
nurture my love of cooking and travel and end up a food writer.
I'm fortunate to be doing what I love for a living but there's
a wrinkle – I'd eaten my way into a prison – one that made
movement in general much more labored than it needed to be

(no surprise there). Even sleeping and sitting are considerably more difficult at 300 pounds-plus. My body longs for freedom and ease but I have no clue how to get there. Certainly dieting is out of the question, as is gastric by-pass surgery. I know friends who have had success with it, but my body's intuition rules against it as not the right choice for me. In December of 2008 I decide to make peace with my life once and for all and two weeks later, the hand of Providence intervenes. It's the proverbial case of the student being ready and the teacher appearing. Cliche as it sounds, sometimes the most significant roads in life really do lead to Oprah. After seeing Carnie Wilson interviewed on the Oprah Winfrey show on January 5, 2009, I tracked down Diamond Dallas Page, the fitness guru who helped her get healthy from the inside out. Through DDPYOGA and its online support community, I meet an amazing and compassionate woman named Terri Lange who has transformed her life and her soul through self-care, patience, and good old-fashioned discipline. Terri and Dallas himself see that I'm serious about this journey and they agree to mentor and support me. I sensed immediately this is a solid solution based in truth…there wasn't even the faintest whiff of snake oil anywhere on the horizon, so I agree to place some trust in them, while retaining the counsel of my own wisdom and intuition (something I've learned should never be ignored or shoved to the back of the bus). I dive in. I'm ready to listen and learn new things. Terri and Dallas offer advice on nutrition. I try It on for size and discover that it's useful. My body commences releasing weight at a safe and steady pace and it's not a struggle. I'll repeat this part because it is vastly profound: The release of weight from my body is not a struggle this time. It is natural and there's no existential whipping or unreasonable deprivation involved. It happens with a rather remarkable flow. And this does not mean it's a quick or easy process. There is effort involved…anything worth having requires effort and I'm good with that. As important as food choices and movement are to well-being and transformation, there's another golden key: the tending of the soul, that's an inextricable part of the process. I begin to write about it on my blog and in newspaper essays. Word trickles out. People who have lost hope are encouraged. I'm encouraged. Especially by reader mail such as this letter from a woman:

Dear Stacey –
I hope I can find what works for me soon. Personally, I think you are making such great progress because you have done the very hard internal work necessary to overcome that heart hurt that keeps us all from respecting and loving ourselves enough to really care for ourselves.

This spectacular lady hit it on the head. I have done the hard inner work. I had to. I had to be my own advocate in a world that said I wasn't deserving of dignity or respect because of my size. The transformation process had to include me believing... knowing that I'm a valid human being no matter what size my jeans are or what the scale says. It's amazing how life can shift when you summon the courage to question the status quo. I could have gone on believing society's crazy beliefs such as Marilyn Monroe is a bit on the chubby side. It took a considerable amount of will and unflinching courage to swim upstream. But at long last I was able to see that I have a choice stay unhappy and undeserving or kick my way out of it. You know what this means, don't you? If anyone's dumping on you now, question it. I did, and it saved my life. I don't know if I'd still be alive if I didn't intervene on my behalf. It was that dire.

Now – Thanks to doing the inner, the outer was finally able to welcome the healing forces that led to a 180-pound weight drop. Being 12 sizes smaller hasn't erased pre-existing problems from my life but GOD it feels great to be free physically! Losing the equivalent of three runway models (and having 20 inches disappear from my hips) doesn't mean pain and problems don't arise. C'mon, you know better than that. Just last week I had some painful stuff crop up out of nowhere and push my buttons like they haven't been pounded in years. The difference is now, I process the pain rather than bury it in an avalanche of simple carbs. I still get the occasional 'so what's your goal-weight question from women who assume I'm dissatisfied with myself because I don't wear sleeveless mini-dresses. And there will always be men who view life as a wet t-shirt contest just waiting for them to judge it. As for me, I couldn't be more OK with who I am…inside and out.

Epilogue: In the spirit of loving myself no matter what the scale says, I'm posting an old picture from my 40th birthday. I'm well over 300 pounds…and know without question my true worth.

The Fat Girl's Dilemma: Finding Friends Who Are Real

I get mail all the time from people wanting to know how I dropped nearly 200 pounds and kept it off. Understandably, they want answers so they can apply the same techniques to their own lives. Most expect a prescription that involves me telling them what to eat. They want details on calorie ranges, protein-carb ratios, daily fat gram allotments, etc.

Instead, and in the interest of being true to my story and how I did it, I begin by telling them what NOT to eat. And the

suggestion has nothing to do with food. Healing for me began in earnest when I decided one day, circa the year I turned 40, that I would no longer be the willing recipient of crap. That's right: No more eating it. As a fat kid turned obese adult with a crippling desire to be accepted, I'd been on a steady diet of crap-taking for decades, and I'd had

enough.

You see, it was the ingestion of cutting remarks, judgmental glances, and outright insults that were really responsible for the weight. The potato chip binges were just a means to quelling my rage and salving my hurt feelings. What was really responsible for the pounds piling on was me accepting mistreatment from others and pretending to be OK with it.

Sure, it hurt when a stranger was mean to me simply because they didn't approve of the way I looked. But what injured me to the core is when the vitriol came from members of my inner circle, or as some of them liked to call themselves... my "friends."

I qualify with quotations because I finally broke through the wall of denial and woke up to the fact that anyone who claimed to love me and care for me would not deliberately insult or hurt me. My size sometimes proved to be an irresistible target, even for those who professed to care for me. I can hear some of you gearing up your battle cry for the "What about the health issues?" argument, but let's get real. If health were a valid concern, you'd also be badgering your friends who smoke, drink immoderately, and go on spending binges, and I never saw that happen. Instead, the only time these sanctimonious ones would mount the high horse was to recite grave would-be statistics, like me being at risk for high-blood pressure, diabetes, and an early grave if I didn't do something about my weight NOW... and by the way, how's your latest diet going?

I'm not denying health risks can be a factor, but I also had to go with my gut every time a lecture or invasive remark came my way, because they were delivered with an unmistakable cloud of antipathy, and not empathy. Because the tradition started so early in my life, I grew to expect the critiques as my lot to live with and was under the shame-induced belief that I had no rights where speaking up for myself was concerned.

School years were the genesis, with mean girls who lacked

emotional maturity laughing and shouting names at me. Sometimes, when my close friends were in a random mood to lash out, who was the easiest target? Why, the largest target in the room, of course.

Anyone else out there familiar with The Fat Girl Drill? You're part of a demographic that's universally looked down on, so run for cover. Compounding the emotional Molotov cocktail is the perception that the fat girl deserves the crap storm because it's her fault she's fat in the first place. Just stop overeating and go on a diet... any idiot can figure that one out. Actually that's largely untrue. If a diet were what I needed, the first one would have worked and I wouldn't be writing this essay.

The true healing of an emotional eater takes years. No one want to hear that, but it's the truth. And when I realized I could diet no more forever, I started to heal the things that really mattered. Like friendships. Since you don't have to be Freud to figure out that the quality of your relationships sing volumes about who you are and how you view yourself, I got to work.

Out went the phony friends whose primary reason for being in my proximity was to look down on me. It took me more than a few years to admit this ugly truth about human nature to myself: there are, roaming the earth, predatory and emotionally stunted people who seek the company of those in compromised situations in order to feel unblemished and superior. I fired those friends, one by one. Some evacuated on their own when it became clear I would no longer be dining on their pseudo-caring lectures and remarks. Others straightened up and decided to fly right, and they were allowed to stay. And the newfound confidence meant an influx of wonderful new friends who didn't care if I was 330 pounds or 130 pounds.

As I was digging through old photos the other day I came across one of me and my friend Stan. He loved and accepted me exactly where I was. He saw and embraced all of my qualities: a great listener with a fabulous sense of humor; also a passionate writer, who is sensitive, impatient, intelligent, and fat. And that's a problem because...? If you cross someone off your list of potential friends because of their weight, please get into therapy, or return to it. You've got some work to do.

With Stan, I never felt apologetic or shameful of who I was. And I NEEDED this. My soul needed it, and so did the broken and betrayed heart of the little girl who just wanted to feel accepted. I needed a friend like Stan far more than I needed to count calories and fat grams. It was a phase that was absolutely crucial to my healing and emotional evolution. And of course, it had to precede any physical healing.

Take a look at the photo of us, and zero in on how Stan is looking at me. At that moment in time, what would you say I needed more: a boot camp DVD complete with seven-day food plan, or the simple, resonant feeling of being loved?

For Those Who Have No Clue...
This One's For You

Why doesn't that out-of-control pig just stop eating?

Helllooo? Just push yourself away from the table – it's simple.

Or my favorite cut-and-dry prescription: Whack your portions in half and start exercising.

Those who have no clue about the inner workings of a person of size piously say phrases like these aloud or to themselves while disdainfully assessing a person of size. And in the interest of not playing games with ourselves, let's come clean and admit the negativity's root: a visceral response to appearance.

If health concern is your argument, please don't use it unless you're also vocally disdainful of the habits of habitual drinkers, smokers, and shop-a-holics. For the 20 years I weighed in excess of 300 pounds, I was more than familiar with disapproving remarks and reproachful looks. As a survival tool, I unconsciously developed an invisible 'back away from the fat chick' force-field around my parameter. Most of the time, a withering look from me was enough to put a would-be lecturer in their place, but a few of the well-meaning health-mongers crashed the gates to dispense some "It's so simple if only you'd just…" pearl of great price…as if they had just helped me crack the wall of the most potent secret since the Da Vinci Code. If only they had a little more information and a lot more compassion, they may have been able to connect the dots a little differently.

Pushing yourself away from the table is fine and good if you're the average Joe or Sally who have slowly let 15-20 pounds creep on due to 'that's life' factors such as middle age, a sedentary desk job, and perhaps a few too many complex carb choices that dot our fast food nation.

But for someone like me, who carried 180 extra pounds on her frame, eating wasn't just eating. It was a psychologically loaded activity. How could I just abruptly cut the cord that connected me to emotional salvation? The answer is, I couldn't. Any attempts I made at an abrupt disconnect via calorie-counting, pre-packaged meals, metabolism-enhancing pills and other Molotov cocktails always ended in a steaming pile-up of a mess.

For those fortunate enough to never have been ensnared in this sort of trap, think of it this way: It's kind of like your arm being on fire and looking for a bucket of water…food is that bucket. Some of you reading relate to this while others are shrugging, wondering why a simple visit up on the roof isn't enough to quell stress on those days when the world is too much to bear.

That's the eternal mystery. I don't have the time or expertise to debate the issue of nature vs. nurture, but let me be clear about the simple truth that people of size don't need your judgment or your two cents, whether in the form of a mini-lecture or a book. If being unhappy with my size, or breaking into a cold sweat at the prospect of fitting into an airplane seat, or feeling disgusted with myself after yet another dieting attempt failed were any kind of valid motivation, obesity would be wiped off of our nation's map. For decades, I directed copious amounts of disappointment and disgust at myself. But it wasn't enough to turn the tide. It really only escalated my defense mechanism of eating to sedate.

People write to me confessing they want to do what I've done but "can't stop" with the food. I know exactly where they're coming from. After my 475th attempt to force myself to be a good girl, a modest eater, a person who was dispassionate about Eggs Benedict and potato salad, I finally waved the white flag and admitted my efforts were not only futile, but probably even detrimental to my mental health. A decade ago, when I was riddled with rage and frustration over a toxic job I'd remained in for about eight years too many, the orange Tupperware bowls full of homemade potato salad carted from my refrigerator to the office probably prevented me from committing a homicide or two. See? Even destructive habits can have a silver lining. I'm not suggesting I was happy with my size or the way my misusing food was siphoning my mental and physical energy. Binge-eating was an automatic habit and coping technique that wasn't in my best interest for a variety of reasons. And speaking of reasons, I decided it was time to start listing the ones that led to me reaching for potato chips and clam dip in the first place. I guess you could say it was a commitment ceremony of sorts, a sacred vow between the self I projected to the world and the humiliated fat girl who kept all her true emotions locked up inside her.

A lot of people don't want to hear this next part, but healing

4

from the inside out was a long process and a journey that doesn't really ever end. It's the nature of life's bumpy road. But wouldn't you rather hear truth for a change instead of lies and manipulation from someone with a financial agenda? The good news is, if you're ready to begin, it's more simple and freeing than you ever imagined. The process of healing from the inside out is actually ready and waiting to unfold...all it requires is activation from you. And there are no hidden fees or membership dues.

The Underrated Verb Known as Admitting

I'm not Jewish, but there's nothing like an honest new year's appraisal of myself and how I can do better in the coming year. If I were sitting in a temple on Yom Kippur, what mistakes would I be acknowledging?

Now, in terms of character flaws, I've committed some serious infractions. Most of them took place during my eating years when, numbed out from overeating and on the lam from reality, I tended not to care whose feelings I'd shred to ribbons if my mood happened to be a foul one... and often it was.

To rid myself of such awful tendencies took time, discipline and a willingness to mature emotionally. And I'm not saying I don't have my cranky and irate moments, but nowadays, I choose to temper my reactions and refrain from lashing out at others. In essence, I've given up the lower-nature practice of hurting people just because I can.

Like one of my spiritual role models, Shirley MacLaine, I've spent most of my adult years smoothing out all the personal shortcomings I can find (except the ones I don't notice). For the

25

most part, my life and relationships are a pretty smooth road. But what still remains in terms of remorse? As I dug a little deeper into my psyche, I realized there's an unhealthy habit I still cling to which oh-so-subtly harms me and those I care for. And in a year's time I'd love to be rid of it for good: I don't tell people how I feel. And by that I mean the good stuff.

I look back on some of the relationships that mattered most to me, whether it was my parents, a favorite babysitter or teacher, my Aunt Mary, a college friend or an editor who made my writing better, and I feel the sting of omission.

I'm not saying a gushy stream of "I love yous" is everyone's style. It isn't mine either, but that doesn't mean I couldn't have expressed feelings along the lines of affection, gratitude and admiration that were silent but swirling below the surface like an underground geyser.

I wish I knew why vocalizing positive sentiments feels so awkward to me. I've gotten better at it, but difficulty still plagues me. If I were even occasionally more open with the people closest to me, there is a very high probability that they would be stunned at the verbal bouquet of glowing adjectives about them that flowed from my mouth.

If I'm being honest with myself, the reality is, I'm simply not comfortable with it... and by "it" I mean aligning my head with my heart, which always seems to be brimming with an open-armed kind of love and doesn't know the meaning of being critical.

Instead, I tell myself it's a safer option to hide the colorful, love-giving and velvet-tender part of me... God forbid I should look foolish. But I'm nearing my fifth decade and what good has it done to shield something so potentially beneficial behind an armor of indifference? Or the armor of, "I'll tell her how I feel in next year's Mother's Day card?"

Next year's never a guarantee anyway.

My father and I always had a somewhat rocky, Ralph and Alice dynamic in our 40-plus years as a father-daughter unit. We tended to communicate in a way that sounded a lot like bickering. And for the most part it was good-natured bickering, but still, but the tone established between us became both a habit and a convenient covering to some of my deeper rooted feelings for him, specifically, that I silently adored him.

There's no truth serum like the shadow of death, and when my beloved Aunt Mary was diagnosed with pancreatic cancer and given six months to live, you can bet I spent as many hours as I could at her side, and told her in no uncertain terms what she meant to me. And last September, as my Father's decade-long ordeal with Alzheimer's was coming to a close, I knew it had arrived: a minutes-long window of opportunity to take a wheel-spinning, Thelma and Louise-style risk or let the moment fizzle and pass into eternity.

Heaving out a sob, I decided to let the armor drop, relieved as it finally clattered to the ground. Then I gripped his hand and kissed his left temple. "I haven't wanted to admit," I whispered. "how much I'm going to miss you."

The producers of Thelma and Louise never did reveal the final fate of the movie's heroines as they triumphantly drove their getaway convertible off a cliff. The frame froze and they hovered magically in midair. I'd like to think the two trailblazers had a Chitty Chitty Bang Bang style of an ending, soaring off towards the clouds instead of plunking to the bottom of the Grand Canyon. Because that's exactly how I felt in those final moment with my father. And actually, it's how I feel every single time I'm real with someone.

So I'm pledging allegiance to my feelings of admiration, love an respect this Yom Kippur, asking forgiveness for all the times I le the moment of truth die and promising to do better this year...

27

especially to those who matter most to me.

Rising and Living

Denial was a big part of my life back in the days when I weighed in excess of 300 pounds. In order to deal with the physical and emotional burden caused by the extra weight I carried around for more than 20 years, my strategy was to plunge, swan-dive-style, into an infinity pool of denial. My self-constructed La-La Land was not just over my size. I also didn't want to confront, in any way, two situations in my life which needed immediate attention: a job that centered around a stressful, negative and emotionally-debilitating work environment, and a 15-year relationship that had dragged on for about 14 years too long. My conscious mind was glib, playing its usual smoke-and-mirrors tricks that said life wasn't all that bad, and I wasn't all that unhappy. But on a gut level I knew I was fooling myself. Not surprisingly, I often told my gut to shut the heck up back in those days. Wow, did I pay a price. Not just in pounds, but in sadness, frustration and spending a large part of my life nearly feless.

I may appear cheerful in this 2003 Mardi Gras photo, but it was my smile, not the green rhinestone mask, that was the real disguise. Looking back, this position of passivity, of being overwhelmed by my personal life, was a big part of why I gave up and accepted that I'd be 300 pounds plus for the rest of my days. If the pain wasn't going anywhere, then neither were the copious amounts of food required to tranquilize myself into a state of what I thought was bliss. And I made sure I had elaborate supplies of junk and fast food at all times, just in case the anesthesia started to suddenly wear off. It wasn't the perfect plan, but it was the only plan I had for dealing with life and all its complexities.

And then life (as it often mercifully does) pulled the rug out from underneath my carefully self-constructed comfort zone. The job got more and more toxic, which turned out to be manna from heaven in the long run, because I finally gathered the courage to permanently evacuate and never look back. The year was 2004, and it was truly a turning point in my belief system, a declaration to the world of what I did and didn't deserve.

Now, about that long overdrawn relationship... I knew when I left the job at Misery Central I still had one more major stone to heave off of my chest, but I chose complete submergence in my favorite infinity pool for another five years, thinking that if I just looked the other way, I could get away with ignoring the issue. But the day came when even a master craftsman of denial like me had to finally look in the mirror and admit I was half alive and bound by the lies I was living.

And while we're on the subject of lies, here's a big one: that people of size will be miraculously cured of what ails them simply by eating less and moving more. Sure, there's physical validity to the formula, but if obesity was solely a physical problem, diets and exercise gadgets would have eradicated the condition off the face of the earth. I had some serious inner wounds to heal. So I tended to them faithfully. When I was eventually ready to start fine-tuning food choices, I went for an intuitive approach. The last thing I wanted was another diet or anything that felt like one. So, in addition to eating when I'm hungry (and not to fill an emotional hole), long-distance walking, yoga and a little dumbbell lifting, I also practice confronting problems and troubling emotions head-on. It's the only way I know to keep both the weight and emotional burdens off my back.

In celebration of the new me, I had a friend take a new Mardi Gras snapshot. Comparing the 2003 photo with the current one, the physical changes are obvious. I'm also different in many ways that will never be tangible, but I feel them. In every moment of every day, I feel them.

The Bullies Are Always Wrong

No one is meaner than a pack of human beings facing someone who is different." - Shonda Rhimes on her childhood spent largely as an outcast.

Now, can I relate to this. And I'm sure many of you can. Because we've been a culture geared for criticizing others rather than scoping out the good in them, there are far too many of us who have had childhoods marked with the sting of degradation and the helpless feeling of isolation.

Anyone who makes it out the other side of this experience eventually connects with the epiphany that the perpetrators were wounded, unhappy people who played the 'look at her not me' game in an inadequate attempt to rise above their own inadequacies. Oh yeah, and the other part of the equation: they were never speaking the truth in the first place. Nothing a bully ever says is enrobed in truth because the core of their message is that their target is defective, less than, and has somehow earned the world's scorn by being 'different.' Their vitriol usually masquerades as labels such as you're too tall, short, fat, thin, dumb, nerdy, or brilliant. Mean boys and girls don't require much in the way of logic to start a campaign.

Case in point: Check out my second-grade self putting on her game face as she heads out the door for the school bus. Once I stepped onto that bus I entered a world where I was told I was fat and therefore, no good. At that particular time, I wasn't fat, but bigger and taller than most of the kids. And even if I was fat, so what? How would that morally or logically correlate to my worth as a human being? Eventually, I went on to become the names and embody the labels. Eating provided a comfortable distraction and temporary amnesia from the humiliation I lived with on a regular basis. When the formative years don't form a healthy sense of self, what results are years of identifying with a falsely constructed self.

Shonda Rhimes went through her school years without the luxury of friends because of her skin color. Her coping technique was to lose herself in reading and writing and she grew into an adult who has become one of the most successful television writers of all time.

It didn't happen overnight, but I awakened to my true self. There's light at the end of the bullying tunnel, I promise. And the wounds do heal, but it takes both work and realization. The day I knew that the bullies were wrong and I was OK all along

was a moment of pure relief, one from which I could make a new beginning. But we've still got work to do, people. Now more than ever it's time to double down and not take the low road when it comes to prejudging others or casting an unkind stone in someone's direction. The older I get the more I look at kindness as a verb. If every action (even thought) sends out a ripple into our world, then let's get a wave going. If we're on this spinning-top of a planet as a unit, then we may as well make the time together as quality as possible. Who's with me?

My New Life

January 5, 2009 is the moment my life changed forever, and not just because I stepped on the scale at my doctor's office and looked down at the numbers instead of away. Looking away from reality was something I'd become expert at by the time I'd reached the age of 44. Nearly four decades of continual practice had me expertly looking through certain elephants in the living room as if they were invisible. Here's a short list:

Dissatisfaction - with the unhappy and unhealthy relationship I'd been languishing in for nearly 20 years

About that abundance of friends – There was nagging evidence, but again, I looked away from the fact that most of my friends were accrued because I was a five-star people-pleaser

The dull ache of sadness – Like a slow heartbeat set at high volume, it pounded from within as I watched my father, for more than a decade, slowly die of Alzheimer's Disease.

The rage - I kept it caged and subdued through chronic carb-ingesting. Deep down, however, I seethed with anger because my coping mechanism carried such a high price tag. The difficulty I had moving through the world, whether it was wedging myself out from under the steering wheel of my car, panting loudly after taking a single flight of stairs, or walking sideways in a crowded restaurant to avoid spilling drinks and knocking tables with my hips.

The numbers…always the numbers on the scale - For 19 years I knew I'd passed the 300 mark, but I wanted no part of knowing exact figures on visits to the doctor. It was enough of a reality check to wear black stretch clothing every day of the year. The numeric specifics I didn't want to hear about.

The abnormality of my eating – And not just the quantity, which was vast, but the choices, which were a study in sugar, fat, and all manner of white carbs, preferably potato chips mounded with clam dip and Italian garlic bread drenched, fondu-style, in melted butter.

I don't recount these details with scorn, especially the last one, because I needed the food to remain sane. For many years, it was the only coping mechanism I had or wanted…and it served a purpose. Until one day, it no longer did. And my Higher Self must have made this realization prior to little old me, because

Suddenly, as I stood helplessly on that digital scale on January 5, 2009, I found myself looking down, and seeing the numbers 345. It was a spontaneous, unplanned moment. It wasn't born of a grand design to take the bull by the horns once again and start a diet. I chose to look at reality that day because something told me it was time. A truth that was reinforced two hours later when I sat sprawled on my chaise lounge with potato chips and dip (my version of a high-ball) and watched an episode of the Oprah Winfrey Show in amazement as a glowing and slender Carnie Wilson spoke of a man named Dallas and how he helped her get her life back.

Carnie's always been my genetic twin and we both fought the weight and size bigotry double-whammy since childhood. Seeing her glowing with happiness was all the impetus I needed for a Google search of her fitness guru. I found Diamond Dallas Page, his DDPYOGA fitness system, and an amazing community of cyber support. I was ready. And not because I was unhappy with my weight. For years I'd hoped against hope that disgust and self-loathing would provide me with the magic bullet of motivation, and of course, it never did.

That's because no positive or lasting change blossoms from negativity. During those 20 years I trance-ate my way through life I decided to give peace a chance. In other words, I knew dieting was futile. I'd done it since age 9 with no lasting results. So why not eat whatever I wanted and simply accept my size and myself. It may sound contrary to logic, but this is exactly what I needed to do after a lifetime of drinking society's toxic Kool-Aid and hating myself with a ferocity that still makes me sad when I look back on it. By the time the calendar said January 2009, my soul had ripened to a point where I knew some physical changes were in order, but they would never define my self-worth. Self-worth, self-acceptance and self-esteem are all treasures that are intangible and by nature transcend weight and appearance. I repeat: your appearance does NOT and never will define your worth. No matter what flashy fantasies those wily industries and lotion-selling con artists are dangling on a stick.

DDPYOGA turned out to be a sound approach to fitness that was designed even for people like me. One look at Arthur Boorman's "Arthur Walks Again" video on You Tube and I knew it worked, but the efficacy of it hinged on my willingness to expend effort. There was no magic, only faithfulness to action. As I began the workouts, I also slowly and non-frantically made changes to my eating habits. Dieting or any of its clever disguises were out. So when my well-meaning nutritionist at the time instructed me to count fat grams, I chucked the advice because I knew it would drive me batty. I was already building positive momentum by cutting out the junk food and concentrating on whole foods cooked at home; that was enough of a change for me to adjust to in the beginning. Also, I'm pretty sure no one ever got chunky by drizzling extra virgin olive oil on their salad. Get what I'm saying?

I learned to rely on my body's wisdom for food choices and quantity. And any time I was drawn to overeat, I remained calm, and rationally recognized that I wasn't screwing up, but demonstrating a reflex-reaction to an emotional sandstorm. I nurtured my emotions as well as my body. And that is probably the biggest tool for me in keeping the weight off. But all of it is important: eating well, moving, feeling…there's no one answer. Yes it's a part-time job, but so was binge-eating, and the trade-off has been more than fair.

These past seven years have been great, but hardly unmitigated bliss. Many longtime friends have slowly faded out of my life or have steadfastly avoided the new me. The truth is, I'd attracted some people who found it appealing to have a fat friend…for varying reasons…I'll leave the analysis to Freud. I mourned the losses (OK, in some cases I rejoiced) and moved on because what can you do? I still worry about my weight when it creeps up, and that's probably never going to end. I also can't eat as much now that I'm at a lower weight and I don't like that because I LOVE FOOD! Aside from that, the only other negative I can think of that stems from being 180 pounds lighter s, I'm much more temperature-sensitive in reverse. In my old life I donned windbreakers in the dead of winter because heavy down overcoats were redundant. Nowadays, I get chilled indoors quite easily. But do you know how EASY it is to reach for a sweater or hoodie vs. trying to cool off at 300 pounds while clad head to toe in black on a July afternoon?

point out the negatives because it's the reality that the diet industry doesn't tell you: weight loss doesn't magically vaporize all the yucky things in your life. The only thing weight loss will do for sure is make you physically freer and lighter (a fantastic feeling if there ever was one) but it's up to YOU to conjure the inner happiness, which by the way, is not a permanent state. I've learned to ride out the emotional storms without food and as a result, they're much tamer in severity and don't keep recurring or haunting my unconscious mind as they did in my eating days.

o here I am 7 years to the day later, nearly 200 pounds lighter, and a whole lot wiser. I hope you'll look at the whole picture I'm giving you. I'm eternally grateful for the turn of events that have helped transform my life. It feels wonderful to wear color, move easily, and not be chained to the habit of ceaseless binge-eating. It was no way to live, and my soul knew that. I had so much help and support from Diamond Dallas Page, Terri Lange, the whole gang at Team DDPYOGA, and my amazing nutritionist, Nancy Guberti. Also true is the fact that I'd done 0 years of inner work, therapy, 12-step meetings, and self-help books to get me ready for January 5, 2009. Preceding the outer transformation was the inner one. I had successfully transformed my belief system to align with the belief that I deserved happiness and supportive, kind people in my life. Believe me when I tell you that back in my 20's I would have swatted anything smacking of goodness away, or assumed it was intended for the person standing behind me.

he weight being gone doesn't mean there aren't days I'd like to get cozy with a bucket of fried chicken or just lounge on the couch doing something constructive like reading (a favorite rationale) instead of working out, but then I stop and do a quickie Q&A. As Dallas taught me, discerning what I want is most helpful in this never-ending journey. Most days I decide I want to remain healthy, energetic, emotionally aware, and physically strong more than I want the momentary pleasure of a binge food or the purported respite from a workout. Most days I choose a protein smoothie over a decadent dessert and unfurl my yoga mat in front of the television instead of sinking into the couch. The truth is, I can read a magazine later, and often I do…but there's power in collective discipline…and 7 years worth has been very, very good for my body and soul.

Denial with a Smile

Every now and then, I find myself missing Lucille Ball, and since "I Love Lucy" reruns aren't on TV often enough, I get my needs met on You Tube, where I found one of my favorite scene from her priceless lexicon of physical comedy: The Vitameatavegamin episode. In it, Lucy realizes her longtime dream of being on TV and schemes behind Ricky's back to be the healthy face for a vitamin elixir. Problems arise when she has to ingest it, spoonful after spoonful while the camera rolls…and make a convincing case for being in love with the way it tastes. Yesterday, as I watched Lucy swallow, wince, and li right through the twinkling smile sh manufactured for the camera, I was struck with revelation: I've played a similar game for years, and it's a big part of why I ate my way to 345 pounds.

Swallowing something I detest and pretending to like it is something I did so many times, it was knee-jerk. It became so automatic; I didn't realize how blithely I tolerated backstabbing bosses and co-workers at a toxic job or an insulting remark from a 'well-meaning' friend.

But nowhere was this coping mechanism more employed than at the molten core of my personal life. Anyone who's familiar with my writing career knows about the opinion essays for magazines, newspapers, and public radio. Many of them dug deep into personal topics that were sometimes painful to reveal publicly: my weight, love-hate affair with food, my father's decline into Alzheimer's, size bigotry. But the one topic I steered clear of was my relationship of nearly 20 years. That's right, I said 20.

You know," a close friend pointed out one day after reading one of my revelation-filled essays. "You treat your relationship as if it doesn't exist." Her words were an awakening thud to the gut 10 years ago. And still, I did nothing about it. Why kick up the mud that I willed so hard to settle at the bottom of my psyche? I thought I'd devised a brilliant way to keep the waters muck-free: Ignore the things that my gut (always golden in its accuracy) was telling me. It's not that I didn't hear my gut when it sent distress signals to my brain. I always hear…but do I pay attention? For 20 years I convinced myself that sexual compatibility, intellectual chemistry, and standing on common moral ground were insignificant over the long haul. Can you imagine the energy this took? It may sound small potatoes but it turned out to be a lot of burden to live with.

This was my Vitameatavegamin: spending nearly half my life with a man I was never in love with. Trite as it sounds, the reasons why I stayed so long were, ahem, complicated. It wasn't a horrible relationship. If he'd been abusive it would have been a no-brainer to leave. There was our Christmas Eve tradition of watching "The Little Drummer Boy" by the light of the tree, both of us crying at the end when the drummer boy's lamb is healed at the manger. The strawberry birthday cakes I baked for him every June. And the 'Very Important Person' certificate he surprised me with in 1992 when I was unemployed and felt like a complete loser. To this day he remains one of the sweetest people to have ever come into my life. And I'll never stop being grateful for the way he was able to love me. During our two decades together he saw me gain an alarming amount of weight. He knew my history of emotional abuse and never once said an unkind word to me about my size. No one, and I mean no one (except my dogs) have given me that kind of unconditional love.

And about that triple-digit weight-gain: part of it I'm sure was me trying to prove that I was unlovable. If I got fat enough, even he would throw in the towel. I don't think he ever would have. But that was only part of the eating equation. My other reasons were to smother the feelings of emptiness that came with being in a romantically loveless relationship. I thought a lot about the validity of simply going through life with a companion. It's a gift that some never get, so why should I complain? Passion is intoxicating, but it fades, it's childish, it's an unnecessary prop. Besides, I wasn't that unhappy. I simply liked food more than the average person. So l lived on Italian bread soaked in melted butter. No one's perfect. It had to count for something that we cared about each other. It did count. But it wasn't enough.

I became pretty good at lying to myself. But there's some sort of gravitational law about truth. It can be sequestered, reconfigured, and smothered, but it has a way of winning in the end. It would pop up in front of my face when I least expected it scaring me like a jack-in-the-box: the photographs of us doing our best to look the part of a happy couple, my escalating binge-eating, his attraction to gambling which had long ago spiraled out of control. Like a lot of couples in crisis, there was the phase where I took refuge in declaring him as the source of all my misery. But he wasn't the problem. It was me and my choice to live a lie.

Then, one day, I did what I thought I'd never have the courage to do: I told him. It was hard, even a little painful. But not nearly a brutal as I thought it was going to be. What I think he was able

o recognize was the simple truth I was putting forth: it wasn't
a referendum on his self-worth, but a declaration that I wasn't
happy. He also knew that I didn't hate him and there was no
other man standing by in the wings, waiting to pull me onto his
stallion and whisk me away to a magically new life under the
protective cover of his cape. And because I was able to finally
admit the truth, it left me able to appreciate him without the
entanglement of pretense. He and I are friends now. Something
I wasn't sure would be possible. It's not always easy. I was born
with a uterus, which means sometimes my sense of duty and
guilt can be exponential. He didn't want our relationship to end
and I know there's a part of him that's hurting because of it.
Sometimes that weighs on me…And there's not much I can do
about that other than live with it.

I'm at peace now with releasing that burden I carried for so
long. Not surprisingly, taking the big risk was followed by a
torrent of weight melting off of me. And while it's a major part
of the puzzle, it's only one. That's what I'm learning through all
of this: health and balance are multi-faceted. I can't just focus on
one area: food, feelings, exercise, relationships, desires, passion,
calories, it's all part of the picture. Knowing which area needs
my immediate attention is a learning process.
Who knows, maybe I could have let it slide for another 20 years,
but I don't think so. January 2009 brought to my doorstep some
profoundly life-changing moments and this was one of them.
Something in me had reached the limit. I couldn't do it anymore
and the time had come to make a choice: Live for me or live
for someone else. Nearly four years later, I've kept the weight
off and am living a life of physical and emotional freedom that
is gratifying beyond words. But the best part is hearing what
people tell me over and over about my eyes: they have life in
them again. Hallelujah. It's about time.

Moving Through Grief

On Sept. 28, my father left us. Peacefully, in his nursing home bed, surrounded by Love. He was in that bed for more than nine years, and afflicted with Alzheimer's disease for 13. Given the circumstances, it might come as a surprise when I say I'm devastated by the loss. Logically, I realize that we lose our parents. The fact that it's a natural part of life doesn't make it any less painful when their death happens, even if it is a merciful end to a lingering illness. My Father and I were extremely close. We dieted together, overate together, struggled with low-self esteem together because of our size. He saw me regain 100 pounds twice. Watching me spiral down a second time was brutal on my Father because he always wanted me to be free. It tears at my heart that he didn't get to experience the joys of my new, transformed self with me.

I've been mourning him for nine years, but now that he's fully gone, the finality of it hurts. I know the sting of loss won't always be as sharp as it is right now. Sometimes I think of him with a laugh. Other times I tear up when I see his framed smile across the room. The truth is, you're never really ready to stop being with someone you deeply Love, seeing their face, hearing them laugh. Facts-of-life logic only go so far at times like these. The Heart has a far different interpretation. And I've been listening, because it's the only way through the forest.

What has this to do with weight loss, fitness, and healthy living? Absolutely everything. File this under the 'how to cope with the emotional triggers that could drive you back to the La-La Land of trance eating' category. I don't want to return La-La Land. For years, binge-eating is how I coped with my feelings of sadness over slowly losing my Father. All it got me was more buried in the muck of unfelt feelings and extra weight. I was slower, heavier, and my senses almost completely dulled. Getting comfort and

elief from binge-eating is an illusion. It never took away any pain
or solved any problem - it only distracted me from an issue, and
hen compounded it.

*So here I sit today at the computer,
throat a little achy from crying, as I
listen to the beautiful chords of
Johann Pachelbel's 'Nocturne,' as
arranged by Michael Maxwell. It
sounds like the music angels would
play, and it was Maxwell's "The
Elegance of Pachelbel" CD that filled
the nursing home room during my
Father's passing. I'm committed to
feeling this stuff, whatever comes
along with the process of grieving. I
want to remain as whole and as alive*
s possible.

*nd I'm also committed to honoring my Father's memory and
he imprints he left on so many during his time on Earth. So here
e is, captured in an essay I wrote for his memorial service on
)ctober 2. He's a pretty cool guy:*

was 1982, the year I was a high school senior. A classmate
ad just pulled into my driveway to pick me up for a shopping
xpedition at the mall. As I slid into the passenger seat, I saw her
)oking toward the house. "Look," she said with a smile "There's
our father." I hadn't noticed, but after saying a quick good-bye
) him at his home office, he must have quietly slipped outside
) the back porch to watch us pull away. He stood in that feet-
rmly-planted stance, jingling change in his pockets, smiling at
s like a benevolent apparition on the elevated deck. I shook
1y head and probably rolled my eyes in mock frustration. "He's
ways gotta oversee every detail," I murmured, noticing that
1y friend looked both intrigued and a little wistful as she gazed
: him. "Well, you're lucky," she said, as she backed out of our
riveway. "I wish my father paid attention to me like that."

Rapt attention. It's what my father gave anything or anyone he felt passionate about, or even a little interested in, whether he was cheering Ronald Reagan in a presidential debate, visiting with a van full of newly arrived Timlo campers, or keeping vigil over a Teflon pot full of Snow's Clam Chowder, heating it to just under a simmer so the milk wouldn't burn. Whether you were a niece or a nephew, his favorite pharmacist, a family friend, or the paper boy, if my Father was fond of you, you would be showered in a zany, effervescent kind of love that left you feeling enveloped in affection.

My Father had many passions in life, and like a multi-faceted jewel, just as many sides to him:

He was the chronic dieter who could steel his determination to exist on poached chicken breasts and bottles of Tab...and the carnivore whose idea of a perfect meal was Prime Rib and Mashed Potatoes at The Montcalm.

He was the Ivy League graduate who came home from church on Sundays to watch the body-slamming shenanigans of Chief Jay Strongbow and Andre The Giant during the weekly pro-wrestling matches on television.

My father had a home office, but loved being on the open road, and had an innate gift for navigating it. Whether it was Baltimore, Miami, or his beloved Pittsburgh, my Father effortlessly made his way through and around frenetic beltways and poorly marked highways like a homing pigeon in the days when GPS devices didn't exist.

His unquenchable thirst for current events was well-documented, and began with morning newspaper headlines, followed by Paul Harvey at noon, and Walter Cronkite at 6:30 p.m. Before bed each night, he'd sit at the kitchen table paring the skin off a whole grapefruit into a perfect coil while Ted Koppel interviewed the latest embroiled heads of state.

My Father was also the perfectionist who liked things just so, such as his morning routine of black coffee poured to the brim of two white ceramic cups, the contents of which he didn't touch until they cooled for 10 minutes. Then he'd gulp them down back-to-back and begin his day.

And probably the most amusing side to him: the unapologetic germaphobe who traveled with cans of Lysol in his trunk and would politely but unmistakably back a few paces away if you sneezed in his presence.

About halfway through writing this, I came to the conclusion that the floodgates of memory had been flung wide open upon my father's passing, and was overwhelmed with the sheer volume of anecdotes, all of which reflected a different glimmering surface of the jewel. He was that colorful and that memorable a man. So I had to narrow it down to a single episode in the 48 years I had with him that summarizes the quality I appreciate most: Compassion.

True to his contradictory nature, my father was a caring man, but found it almost impossible to show it in the form of touchy-feely vocabulary or physical affection. Instead, he called on his masterful powers of intellectual oration when someone was in distress. The way he did on that bleak Saturday morning in the spring of 1980 when I woke to the news that our elderly German shepherd, Duchess, was suddenly failing, and the time had come for that final visit to the vet. Her death left a particularly deep wound in me. Duchess came into my life when I was two, before Dory, Mike, and Jeff were born. She was a tiny bundle of fur when my Father brought her home in late September, 1966, an anniversary gift for my mother, because he wanted a watch dog to protect the home for the times he was away on business travel. For 14 years, Duchess silently trailed me like a guardian angel, and her unexpected departure from our lives that weekend left me too distraught to contemplate writing an essay on Dickens' "A Tale of Two Cities," that was due Monday.

4

Ever the resourceful networker, he tracked my teacher down on Sunday, phoning her at home to explain the situation. He knew English was my favorite subject and it was unlike me not to delve into a reading assignment. I could hear him through the wall of his office, gently but persuasively making a case for a week's clemency to finish the paper, bolstering his point with a brief outline of why Duchess was no ordinary canine to me or the rest of the family. As a first-time conversation with Barr Morris often went, his chat with Mrs. Davies eventually veered off the original subject and soon they were talking like an old friends.

Whether an incident was big or small, my Father couldn't tolerate people hurting. He may not have been comfortable doling out hugs, but if one of us scraped our knee playing outside, he scrambled to the medicine cabinet for the box of Band-Aids and bottle of merthiolate. "This is going to sting a moment," he announced before dabbing the wound with the flourescent pink disinfectant. "But I'll blow on it to make it better." I don't know if it was the cool jet stream of air or his TLC, but the stinging stopped in its tracks each time. And if he knew that a neighborhood kid was being ostracized or picked on, my Father would call a meeting with his us to brainstorm ideas on how we could make the unfortunate one feel better.

He was also a loving Husband, whose tendency to procrastinate never deterred him from coming home on the evening of my Mother's birthday or anniversary with an armful of gifts and a romantic card. As some of you know, my Father left us just a day before their 50th wedding anniversary. It had been years since we'd heard my Father's voice, and I can only guess that, had he been able to express it, he would have had so many things to say to my Mother on the eve of their Golden milestone. Even had it been the old Barr, able to captivate with his melodic speaking voice overlaid with the most carefully chosen and elegant vocabulary, I doubt he would have found the proper words to express his awe and admiration to Margy for her devotion: nine solid years of visits to his room at The Pines, sometimes twice a lay.

A few days ago, as we sat across from each other at his bedside,
 asked my Mother what it felt like to be in possession of an
E-Z Pass through the Gates of St. Peter. She just smiled and
stroked his arm, saying she's done nothing heroic. Loving and
caring for my Father in sickness was never a question or a chore
to my Mother. Theirs was a bond that lasted through some
significant tribulations, even the more minor of which would
likely vaporize many of today's short-term marriages. And last
week, my Father's days were filled with turbo-charged doses of
love from his family, a few close friends who came to say good-
bye, an avalanche of prayers from near and far, and from the
wonderful nurses at The Pines, all of whom had tears in their
eyes when they stopped at his bed to check on him, even if it
wasn't their shift.

Friends reminded me over the years that it's vital to remember
my father as the man he really was. So I like to picture him
presiding over the grill on our deck, wearing his red "Hail To
The Chef" apron as he oversees the charring of steaks for dinner.
I can see him coming off the tennis court, his face beaded with
sweat as he wipes his brow and gulps a paper cup of ice water.
Or standing next to me on the shores of Lake George, peering
through the thick lenses of his navy binoculars to see if the
sailboat in the distance is a Rainbow or a Star.

These past few months, it was clear my Father's time was
approaching. That knowledge caused me to do things like sift
through old photographs and ponder his qualities a little more
deeply. Our physical similarities have always been evident.
From my Father, I inherited blonde hair, pale blue eyes, a
predisposition for sunburning, and a healthier than average
love of fried chicken. But the most meaningful things passed
on are always intangible, and I continue to perfect the ones my
Father gave. Thanks to him, and in spite of existing in a world
that is not always kind, I learned that it is a beautiful thing to
greet people with my Heart instead of my head, that smiling is a

natural state, and that forgiveness is always the better option.

Riding Out The Dark Days

I love my new life now that past wounds are healed and the weight is off. Most days are good, or at least, infinitely better than they were 20 years ago when black lycra was my uniform and my enjoyment of life hinged upon eating large amounts of caloric food, and after I consumed it all, planning the next ritual feast. I had decades to perfect this unhealthy coping mechanism and became very artful at dodging reality. After a few wake-up calls and with dedicated practice, I'm now pretty good and wading through reality, one present moment at a time. I know what you're thinking and BINGO, you're right! Standing firm in the present is a double-edged sword. In order to gain access to the members-only club known as reality, I've agreed to savor the highs and also stop in my tracks to fully experience the disappointments and despair that are part of life's tapestry. When the pain is hardcore, it's a very difficult thing to do, but even so, I prefer feeling whatever's showing up to backsliding.

In the interest of admitting my human condition, backsliding sometimes happens. During an especially trying time in my life, I slipped seamlessly, without realizing it, into my old defense mechanism of playing dead. Flat-lining emotionally was an old trick that got me through the school years: I'd go numb and pretend the bullies and mean girls weren't lacerating my heart with their insults. 'I'm not hurting-It doesn't hurt-I feel nothing' became my silent mantra, and one I thought I'd outgrown until the moment when someone very close to me died suddenly. Tony was my former partner, a spiritual brother, and someone whom everyone close to me in my life loved. For proper backstory on Tony, please refer to the earlier essay, "Denial with a Smile."

I ended our 20-year relationship in 2009, the year that turned out to be the year of reckoning regarding all the denial I'd been living with. Denial only appeared to keep me safe and happy; in reality, it was more like a prison, and my agreement to live within it was not a positive move for my soul. Once the denial was vaporized, my energy was freed to delve into a few things I'd been avoiding, like facing the fractured nature of the relationship we'd both been languishing in. It was excruciatingly difficult to look Tony in the eye and tell him what I needed to do. But my soul could no longer be ignored, so I spoke my truth. We parted as friends and remained in touch, having coffee occasionally and spending holidays together – my family adored Tony and his family was at a distance, geographically.

Following our split, I was thoroughly focused on both taking care of my health and getting to know who I was. I didn't end it with Tony to bounce into the arms of another man, I ended it to reconnect more deeply with me. So what's the problem, you're probably wondering. The problem was, Tony wasn't thriving the way I was after we separated. I knew there was a 50-50 chance of him taking this new chapter and deciding to explore, expand, and experience new things. But Tony didn't take that road and it haunted me that his life revolved around going to a job he disliked and then coming home to an empty apartment. Had I not initiated the lonely life he was experiencing? I felt that part of it was on my shoulders, and things only got worse when, one afternoon after work, he was rear-ended by another car. The injury he sustained to his shoulder required minor day surgery that seemed routine on the surface. A week later, however, Tony had a massive heart attack. It was five years after our break-up and by this point, I was in a relationship with a wonderful man (for backstory on that, see the essay on intimacy). One of Bill's many virtues is being an excellent cook. That first year we were together he invited my family (including Tony) to his home for Thanksgiving. Bill and Tony, it turned out, really liked one another and became friends, much to my delight. Another one of Bill's beautiful virtues: his compassion. With Tony's health in peril, it was Bill who suggested Tony move in with us for some TLC as he convalesced.

The next few months were pretty amazing. Bill and Tony grew closer, we all talked about Tony's new lease on life and how he was going to tackle new places and experiences once he got well Bill cooked incomparable family dinners every night and we'd watch Jeopardy and 'Sopranos' reruns afterwards. On one of those cozy evenings, as Bill reached for his sauté pans, I heard a loud thud in the other room that frightened me. I ran to where Tony was and dropped to my knees to be closer to him. As Bill called 911, life went into slow motion, and all I could think to do was weakly offer Tony the assurance that help was on the way. A police officer arrived within seconds, it seemed, and began CPR. When the paramedics converged with their defibrillators I got out of their way and began praying. By the time Bill and I arrived at the hospital 45 minutes later, my childhood defense mechanism was in high gear. I had gone numb the minute I heard Tony fall to the ground. I felt no pain as a nurse told us Tony was dead. I continued to feel nothing when she pulled the curtain back in the emergency room bay and saw him, lying there like a cement figure. I'd love to say he looked peaceful but he didn't; the struggle of the last 45 minutes showed on his face. I took a seat next to the bed and proceeded as if Tony were still present, tenderly rubbing his stomach they way a mother reassures an ill child. It felt natural for some reason. Perhaps it was my too-little-too-late means of offering comfort after the pain I caused him with the breakup…and all the years we spent together where I wasn't exactly my best self.

Guilt, shame, regret and the like are part of the 'being human' package. The key is not getting stuck in them, and I know how easy it is to hop aboard the hamster wheel of unkind, repetitive thoughts and have that wheel spin me to the dark side. During our time together, I was often miserable, more than a little out of balance, and very unpracticed in the art of compassion. Tony was gentle, easy-going, and a convenient target for my rage. Unhappy, imprisoned by fat, and completely disconnected from truth, Tony saw the worst of me, and tolerated my dark side better than anyone else in my life ever did. If it weren't for his unconditional acceptance of me, I would not be where I m today. He will always be one of the greatest teachers of my ifetime.

The shock reverberations of Tony's sudden death invited the unwelcome and aggressive invasion of my shadow-self. It hovered and taunted, like a 12-foot marauding demon, insisting that I relive my past mistreatment of Tony in unsparing detail. This is the downside of the mind: it can take you to terrible places if you let it, and for a long time, I rationalized that after all I put Tony through, the least I could do was dump on myself indefinitely. And that gave way to the lines between the rieving process and beating myself to a toxic pulp becoming voefully blurred.

his year marks the fourth anniversary of Tony's passing. I still niss my friend, teacher, witness, and soul brother; so does Bill, nd our dog, Sophia, who followed Tony everywhere around he house. Even in death, he continues to teach me. After ears of emotional turmoil, confusion, and pain, I knew it was nperative to take back control of my thoughts and my shadow. d done a thorough job of allowing the feelings, feeling them, ven soaking in them. But I wasn't moving on. It was a defining noment because I had deluded myself into thinking the emorse was calling the shots. I've concluded that unrelenting uilt was an aspect of my shadow that seized an opportunity to ounce and knock me off balance. Egos exist to obsess on the egative. Steering the mind properly and not allowing it to sink ne into a place of hopelessness is one of the great challenges of nis human-brain-existence.

n a nutshell, I had to get very proactive with my stream of egative consciousness and (over and over till it got easier) tell my inner mean girl to talk to the hand. And there were occasions, absolutely, where food became more of a focus and a comfort than it should have been. But Hallelujah, disappearing into binge-eating didn't feel alluring or natural. Seeking refuge in a bowl of clam dip big enough to feed seven would be like hopping back on a wobbly child's bike with training wheels after becoming accustomed to the superior glide of a 10-speed Schwinn.

Maintaining balance takes awareness and action; that truth is a constant in all this. I am grateful to say that I'm giving guilt, shame, and remorse their proper place on the emotional spectrum. I see them for what they are: carriers of valuable information. And I am very clear on this: They do not define me. I am much more than my emotions...and my past.

Negotiating Intimacy: The Truth Not Found in Diet Books

"Is there anything you think would put you in danger of re-gaining the weight?" my good friend Doug asked me one afternoon back in 2011. For much of our lives we both fought the war with the scale, and he knew my history of being a chronic regainer.

The answer I gave Doug was instantaneous. "Yes," I said, leaning forward across the table at lunch that day. "Men."
Seven years ago I was fresh off my most recent victory with said scale: 180 pounds lighter and enjoying an understandably new way of existing. Having learned much from all of my past

weight loss 'failures,' I knew in precise terms what did not work for me, so there would be no more buying into quick-fix seductions from the diet industry. This time, I conquered obesity and binge-eating through a mosaic of solutions: self-help books, therapy, 12-step meetings, meditation classes, even a soul-searching stint in a food rehab. And when the wounds were properly salved, I was ready to take on the physical leg of my journey, finding a form of movement I clicked with (DDPYOGA) and getting nutritional advice from functional medicine specialist Nancy Guberti, one of the best in the business.

There's no magical, easy life once the weight is gone, however. I still had to live with myself...and my hang-ups and fears. 25 years ago a painful break-up sent me reeling. Determined to never be hurt again, I dove head-first into regaining lost weight and hiding from the issues of intimacy. I hid with copious amounts of food and by half-heartedly agreeing to a relationship with a man where I knew I wouldn't be fulfilled or happy, but hey, it was about hiding from the truth, so I was all-in. My body and soul paid the price. It was only after I was aroused from this self-inflicted coma 20 years later that I took a step back and admitted how profoundly unhappy I was. What, did you think lasting weight loss was all about calories in/calories out? If only it were that cut and dry.

But don't be discouraged. Please don't be discouraged. All
it takes is a little bravery. Once you wade into the waters of
honesty you'll discover it's not only not excruciating, it's freeing.
After a year or three of taking time to reconnect with myself
again, it seemed like the right time to think about dating. I
assumed that with the weight off, a roster of dashing men would
somehow find me and commence courting. They didn't. Friends
suggested online dating. I objected, declaring it was for losers
who couldn't meet people on their own. Another year went by
and I still wasn't meeting people on my own. Humbled, I joined
a dating site, knowing it would be more than a viable way to
meet a guy – online dating would provide a golden ticket to face
my fears and slay them once and for all.

Did I experience rejection? Of COURSE! Were some of my
hopes dashed? Yup. Was there a healthy percentage of players?
Affirmative. But a wise friend imparted some powerful
wisdom to me at the beginning of my online search that stuck:
something along the lines of 'no one can make you unhappy
but you.' Sure, people can disappoint me, but it was incumbent
on me to mind my side of the street, properly interpret the
red flags, and not get carried away in my head. And believe
me, I was getting fed up with bob-and-weave shenanigans of
the online dating pool. Perhaps it was time for a break...I was
approaching the six-month mark, and my patience was set to
expire with my membership.

But, at the 11th hour, I grudgingly agreed to one more coffee
date before checking out. January 11 is the day the walls came
down, not because I was invested in a fantasy, but all the years
of trial and error, learning and discerning, and rising again after
each dust-up had taught me well. I sensed goodness in the man
who sat across from me that morning of January 11, 2012, and
as it always is, my gut was correct.

So, cheers to not only 6 years, but to surmounting obstacles
and smashing down walls that keep us hidden. Risks are soul-

nhancing, and disappointment is survivable. This I know for
ure.

- Food -

Dead Dieter Walking

The most memorable scene from the 1996 film "Dead Man Walking" are those few minutes Sean Penn's character has to contemplate his execution. His demise is only minutes away and the pain he exudes in that scene is palpable. The pained expression on his face paints a clear picture that his life, in no uncertain terms, is on the verge of being brought to an end.

Uncountable times, I've lived this dread. Perhaps not quite to the excruciating extent that Sean Penn portrays in the movie, but I'm familiar with the soul-sucking rhythms of the 'dead man walking' ritual. It's the pre-dieting rite of passage that's every bit as bitter as it is sweet. Card-carrying dieters…you know what I'm talking about: (deep breath) *the last meal*. Or, more accurately, the last good meal we'll ever have…a passionate good-bye kiss to the foods we actually *enjoy* eating.

Because it's all about extremes, isn't it? What else is there? What is this thing known as the middle road? I couldn't be trusted with food, so lockdown was imposed. The ironic thing about brute force is, it doesn't work. It doesn't reform prisoners and it doesn't cure dieters of what truly ails them.

The groundwork for extremes was laid early for me – at age 9 when I was put on my first official diet, courtesy of our family doctor, whom I'll refer to as Dr. No. My father loved Dr. No's philosophy because, in addition to a strict, nearly fatless diet, he prescribed a two-day binge to precede the part where we're stripped of dignity and personal freedom. I lost track of how many times my father and I jumped on and off the Crazy-Wheel. But the bulging paper grocery bags we'd haul home after a visit to Dr. No's office were filled with the building blocks of our two-day farewell feast. Things we promised (more damantly each time) we would never eat again: pork chops, potatoes with butter, creamy cascades of Stouffer's chipped beef over toasted white bread, chocolate marshmallow ice cream crowned with a fluffy head of Cool Whip.

8 hours later, the menu did a 180: dry string beans and a soft boiled egg for breakfast; tuna splashed with cider vinegar for lunch; and a dinner of poached chicken breasts and iceberg lettuce. Halfway through the day I was dazed with both hunger and depression.

Why hasn't anyone been more vocal about stating what's obvious: that diets are just plain mean?

I could recite a laundry list of why dieting hasn't worked for me, but probably the biggest clue that they're a monumental set-up for failure is the way they begin: with a 'life is over' implication that's about as appealing as being led to the execution room. Somewhere along the way, I realized that this method (that is still inexplicably embedded in our collective psyche as a viable solution) is really the definition of futility. If dieting could have killed the part of me that loves food, is drawn to it, wrings pleasure from it, dieting would have done it…the first time around. It wasn't until after my second 100-pound gain-back that I decided I would no longer entertain the idea that diets could help me. That was in 1990. Not knowing what else to do, I did what I always did when I wasn't dieting. I ate. A lot. True, I got bigger each year, but not having the schizophrenic agony of the crazed 'in and out/off and on' cycles to contend with brought a welcome sense of peace.

So no one is more surprised than I am that the year 2009 began a torrent of personal transformation that included dropping 130 pounds. This time though, I did it through listening to the intelligence of my body. It's probably hard to believe, but I actually forgot that my body is intelligent. I also did a lot of listening to Diamond Dallas Page, creator of DDPYOGA, as well as Terri Lange, an amazing woman who has kept her weight off for 8 years.

I get asked lots of questions now about how I did it. And last week someone wanted to know if I had a 'last supper.' When I began this new way of eating, this new relationship to food, that didn't even occur to me. In my mind, it would have been too much of an implication that I was beginning a diet. So there was no burgeoning banquet table awash in 'parting is such sweet sorrow' sentiment.

That's because the foods I love have all been invited along for the ride. Yes, I've relegated them to a different position in the pecking order...downgraded their ticket, if you will. But they're still in the picture. It's a full picture now that includes exercise, feeling the feelings, experimenting with new flavors and textures (mashed rutabaga is actually really goooood), and respecting who I am: someone who loves fried chicken. There, I SAID it. Man, it feels good to be out of the closet.

The Head and the Heart: A Peace Accord

In spite of some people finding it unbelievable, I'm sticking with my original story: I dropped a whole lot of weight without dieting. But that doesn't mean I didn't have a plan. I just chose to keep mine loose because my personality type dislikes too much rigidity. I need boundaries and structure, they're essential to progress, but too many absolutes and too few personal choices infringe on my dignity and assume that I have no personal power or intelligence where food is concerned. I once believed, vis-a-vis certain self-help philosophies, that I was powerless and utterly impotent where food and eating were concerned, and that, without a rigid plan, food and all its myriad choices was a towering, fire-breathing version of Godzilla that would level me with a single swing of its tail.

n time and with patience (read: lots of trial and error) I learned
DO have the final say. Which lead me to the magical discovery
f the importance of portion control. Such a logical concept,
nd one I'd resisted tooth and nail for decades. No one was
oing tell me how much to eat — NO ONE! For years I'd not
nly bristle, I would become enraged at the idea of eating till
was satisfied but not stuffed. It's also important to note that
hese were the years I was in emotional crisis: In possession of
oth a toxic job and unhappy relationship, I was also helping to
are for my ailing father. I'd begin each day with two bagels: one
nounded with cream cheese and the other loaded with butter.
ach bite was infused with the only joy I'd be encountering at
ny joyless job and later, after a 9 or 10-hour day, I'd come home
vith either a pizza or bucket of fried chicken. Both served as an
nexpensive high to keep me company in front of the TV until
dragged myself off to bed and began it all the next day. More
agels, donuts, cheeseburgers, all-you-can-eat buffets. On the
urface, it seemed that the food was whipsawing and controlling
ne. A food addict, a psychiatrist might surmise. Not exactly.
was the feelings of euphoria, comfort, and relief, however
emporary they were, that had me in their spell. If I wasn't eating
ood, I was planning my next adventure with it. I enjoyed the
ood I corralled and devoured, tremendously. My tastebuds
vere happy, just about all of the time, but my body bore the
runt of my decisions: Carrying 300 pounds + around was a
urden that drained my vitality. My life was a broiling mess, and
ne comfort-eating was actually needed for me to survive my
ircumstances. Intellectually, I knew food wasn't the answer, but
was in too deep to simply "Just Say No" to the Little Debbie's or
ne Cheetos.

his next part is vitally important for anyone seeking a solution
) the overeating/excess weight dilemma, or else you're probably
oing to continue attempts at fixing the situation with a food
lan or calorie counting: Start working on what you can fix. If
very fiber of you wants to comfort yourself with food, let it
e. I'm telling you from experience that's too big a monster to
ime in quickie women's magazine-style. You'd have better luck

getting Godzilla to heel and roll over using a poodle leash. Work instead on your innards: How are you speaking to yourself? Are you kind and patient, or are you vicious and demanding? What's getting under your skin... or who? Is there anyone you need to stand up to or set a limit with? That's scary stuff... and it used to send me running to the chip aisle of the nearest supermarket or gas station. Are there people you're lashing out at or mistreating because of your own state of unhappiness? It may be time to face it and own up to behavior that is harming others, and ultimately yourself.

These were all things I tackled, one at a time, with courage (because a lot of the time I was shaking with fear as I took the leap), and always with support of understanding friends and family members. I tackled them because 1) They needed my attention and could no longer be ignored, and 2) I wasn't ready or able to start redefining my relationship with food. The inner work took years. Let's be real, it's never really over. But I got to a point where I'd done enough healing and eradicated enough demons that I no longer needed piles of food to pinch-hit for inner peace and happiness. Then and only then could I think about the practice and philosophy of eating till I was satisfied but not stuffed. I was ready to consider eating until my hunger was gone and before my stomach felt overly full. Once that became more familiar I found myself enjoying my increased energy, and marveled at how I no longer needed to lie down after a meal to ease the discomfort in my distended stomach. The work I put in to easing my emotional and psychological burdens meant a gradual diminishing of the edible anesthesia.

Emotional distress comes and goes now. I deal with it as it arises, and it's kind of like drop kicking a tiny gargoyle out of the house. Tiny gargoyles are SO much easier to boot out of one's life than a thundering, fire-spewing Godzilla.

And on those occasions, like a recent brunch, when a bountiful plate of food is put in front of me, I'm able, without a lot of hemming and hawing, to do the following: eat a little more

han half of a gorgeous, delicious, three-egg omelet stuffed
vith sausage, caramelized onions, and melted Manchego. I
lidn't continue to eat past the point of fullness, which meant
10 probability of fat storage. And I continued to reinforce the
ruism to my psyche that I no longer need to eat for three in
rder to be happy.

he rest of the omelet went into a storage container to be
njoyed at a later date for lunch or a snack. I've kept the physical
urden off for almost a decade and this is how I do it. There's no
nagic drink or superfood supplement or diet trick du jour. Just
steady, committed path to healing my inner wounds, listening
o my body rather than ignoring it, and practicing moderation.
ure it's some effort. But I'd rather be free.

Is it Accurate to Call it Cheating?

Within the unofficial country club of former overeaters who
ave dropped and kept off 100+ pounds for five years or more,
here's no shortage of debate as to how it's best done. Some swear
y cheat days while others feel more at ease with a scheduled
heat meal. Still others disavow any sort of deviating from the
lean and narrow and opt for 100 percent commitment to food
hoices that Dr. Andrew Weil and most wellness spas would
reen light. Ultimately, it has to boil down to what works for
ach individual because how else could it be lived with year after
ear?

1 maintaining my nearly 200-pound weight loss, I find it
rucial to walk a fine balance between the worlds of wanton
reedom and iron-fisted discipline. As a lifelong dieter and
inge-eater, I've lived in both worlds and I really don't enjoy
ither of them. So I found a middle road, and would you be
urprised to know that I have my dog to thank for it?
)

When I was two years old, my father got my mother an unconventional but practical wedding anniversary gift: a soft and cuddly German Shepherd puppy they named Duchess. Since my father was a frequent business traveler and we lived in a rural area (eons before the existence of the internet and cell phones), my dad reasoned that Duchess would one day grow into excellent protection for the home and property while he was away.

And she did, quite happily. Duchess's only required compensation for security services was heaping portions of Gravy Train kibble for dinner and a mid-day snack of Top Choice. Despite her pedigree, my father thought it best that Duchess undergo formal training before officially signing on as the family protector. So she endured six weeks of sleep-away obedience school where Duchess was taught the finer points of sitting, heeling, advancing forward and stopping on command. And she absorbed the lessons like a prodigy, executing her newly acquired skills with such precision, we started to wonder if Duchess missed her calling for the Secret Service.

My childhood home was set on about 10 acres of hilly land that was bordered by Adirondack woods. Duchess always roamed the 10 acres freely, because with her innate grasp of obedience, hard-line control wasn't necessary. When we wanted her back closer to home, we'd simply shout out her name and Duchess would come trotting back. Except on those few occasions that she would disappear into the woods beyond our property. The first time it happened I was distraught, thinking she was gone for good. But a few hours later, Duchess came wandering back from the forest across the road a little worn out, but unmistakably happy. It was the canine version of going off on a bender.

Eventually I got the rhythm down. Every so often, say, three or four times a year, Duchess would start walking down the driveway with a purposeful gait that said, "I'll be gone a while." She aimed to take some downtime in the woods just for her, and if anyone calls for her to come home, she's not hearing it. Years later, I finally understood the ritual. Duchess was an obedient, order-following, house-protecting sergeant for 90 percent of the time. But there were days when she just needed to have some dog time and let her hair down. And why not? Wildness and exploration were embedded into her genes. So off she'd go into the wilderness. If it was a good day, she might kill something, or at least give the four-legged creature one heck of a chase. One time she returned with a Santa's beard of embedded porcupine quills. But Duchess never gave up her ritual. And we never asked her to. Being wild and spontaneous was part of her make up. And the 90-10 arrangement was more than fair. Giving up those occasional splurges would have been too much to ask.

It was that childhood nugget of wisdom passed on to me by my first and most beloved dog that actually propelled me to a new level of emotional and physical healing where food was concerned. Don't see a connection? I'll explain: As a chubby kid who became a fat teenager and eventually an obese adult, I was run ragged by the dieting theory that said in order for me to make a permanent change with my weight, I must be forever rigid. And it wasn't just the dieting industry -- 12-step programs, self-help books, celebrity "you too can be as hot as me" memoirs all had a common denominator: Not ONE of them mentioned anything about enjoying fried chicken every now and again. If fried chicken doesn't do it for you, simply insert favorite food of your choice. Ice cream leaves me cold in more ways than one, but if I had to live with the prospect of never eating fried chicken again, I might seriously consider donating my organs to science and calling it a day.

OK, I'm being hyperbolic, but you get the picture. Anyone who's ever dieted knows the depressing grimness of the prison. It's awful. And virtually impossible to live in long-term. I knew six years ago if this attempt at shedding weight and getting healthier were to get off the ground, I'd have to do things differently. One of the first changes I made was to legalize fried chicken. But that change came in tandem with coming to terms with quality and quantity. And frequency. It was to be a special occasion. A treat. And not an escape hatch from life or uncomfortable feelings. And from here on out, the fried chicken would be eaten solo or with a side of vegetables instead of the usual biscuits and butter. And yes, there are times when I decide to be parental with myself and really assess the situation and the desire. If it doesn't feel right, I always take the 'not now' option.

Conventional wisdom says that things like pizza, fried chicken, ice cream, and cake, are nutritionally vile and calorically offensive. Perhaps. But one thing I've learned about myself: I can't eat solely for nutrition all the time, just as I can no longer eat solely for pleasure as I once did. I'm a big believer that it's what you do 80-90 percent of the time that counts. The addict in me had to agree to the revelry being limited to occasionally. In exchange, I learned to like healthy foods and make them my norm. My palate now gravitates to things like lentils, lemon water, steel cut oats, sautéed fish, scrambled eggs, and cauliflower hash. It's all very nutritious and tastes quite good. But my tongue knows its not fried chicken, or my favorite clam dip (which I now make a clean version of with vegan cream cheese).

So on the occasions I've carefully decided to go on a little bender and just, you know, have some FUN with my tastebuds, I offer a simple explanation to those unfamiliar with my philosophy: "Don't be alarmed," I assure them as I scan the shock in their eyes... the shock that's saying, 'You're eating THAT and you're rocking a triple-digit weight loss??"

"No really, don't be alarmed, I'm not spiraling down. I just need go and be a German Shepherd."

~ *Physicality* ~

Confidence Is The New Skinny

Not long ago, I came across an intriguing philosophical statement while shopping for workout clothing online: A black shirt that bore a hot pink declaration that "Strong Is The New Skinny." Loved it. Even if I still take issue with 'skinny' as being an enviable state. What I didn't really dig was the fact that the shirt was sleeveless. I haven't worn anything sleeveless in public since The Brady Bunch aired every Friday night.

 Weighing 300-plus pounds for 20 years meant an unchanging wardrobe of billowy, long-sleeved tops and spandex leggings with plenty of give. I never considered myself to be self-loathing fat women, but I also wasn't comfortable baring skin. Here's my confession: even though I made an avocation out of being confident and self-accepting during the heavy years, I was never one of those big girls who had the courage to wear above-the-knee skirts or tank tops.

As a survival strategy, and because I long ago decided self-recrimination wasn't the answer, I learned to hold my head high when entering a room, even if it meant I was the biggest one present, which I usually was. But revealing my upper arms? Unthinkable. I felt tremendous shame at their overstuffed size. And guess what? Up until this morning I still did.

may have dropped 180 pounds through DDPYOGA, tending to my soul, and clean eating, but my upper arms never got the memo. I've got a pair of bat wings capable of hand-gliding me off a cliff to sail on the wind currents. And I don't say this as a put-down, it's just a fact...and one which may be mitigated one day if I keep up the clean eating, DDPYOGA, and other forms of exercise I indulge in regularly. However, I refuse to let a little residual flab be an excuse for unhappiness. What sense would that make?

There was something about the beauty and sassiness of that black and fuschia tank top that stopped me in my tracks and forced me to no longer hide from my upper arms. As I placed the order and hit 'send,' I knew that this was a shirt I'd be unveiling in the light of day, whether it was on a walk through the neighborhood, hoisting dumb bells at the gym, or rifling through bunches of fresh kale at the farmers market.
This morning, I wore it to a hot yoga class, a place where virtually all shapes and sizes of people are grunting and sweating on their mats...all of them attired in sleeveless shirts. For a month, I suffered through the 90-degree classes wearing 3/4 sleeve shirts. This morning, I showed up dressed like everyone else, realizing it was time to give up the old beliefs of how I should look, time to give up the shame, and time to just start being who I am in this particular moment. To mark the confidence-filled occasion, I even, for the very first time, lay my mat in the front row. I had nothing to hide. It was OK to be front and center. For decades I followed, like a catatonic sheep, the 'beauty' industry's directive of how I should look. Well guess what Shape, Self, Elle, and all the others...THIS is how I look. Period. No explanations or apologies.

Of all the e-mails I get from readers, the number one question by far is from women who are at the start of their journey, and already in a pre-panicked state over having loose skin when the weight's gone. This concern has always puzzled me for a number of reasons:

1. If you haven't gotten to the end of the road yet, you don't really know what the outcome will be.

2. If you don't take drastic measures, like crash dieting or bariatric surgery, the weight will come off at a safe pace and loose skin won't be as likely.

3. Regular exercise tightens muscles and skin.

4. Even if the worst-case scenario pans out and you have (gasp!) loose skin...wouldn't you rather have that than the burdonsome 50, 100, or 200 extra pounds you were saddled with?

This I know from experience: All the years I wasn't ready to stop binge-eating and take an honest look at myself, I'd look (often subconsciously) for any excuse in the book to sabotage plans to clean up my life and get the weight off.

If you've decided that loose skin is too big a risk or too hideous an imperfection to live with, then I'd say you aren't ready. No judgments. Just be honest with yourself about it. I wasn't ready for years. I dropped the weight when I'd done copious amounts of inner healing and practiced self-love until I was fluent in it. For decades I would not and probably could not give up the binge-eating. But I started with movement. If that's all you're able or willing to do, that's PERFECT. Start with walking... or DDPYOGA in your living room if you prefer privacy. But movement will begin to heal you on all levels.

On the biggest, most fat-retaining parts of me, I have loose skin where there were once pillows of fat. My upper arms and inner thighs are not areas I'm enamored with, but I don't dwell on them. Why would I? I'm 180 pounds lighter. I'm immeasurably freer. I'm leaps and bounds happier because I can move easily and without embarrassment. Last night I had dinner in a crowded restaurant where the tables were only inches apart from one another. Five years ago I would have broken into a cold sweat knowing that taking a seat would mean knocking a

...able or two askew. Believe me, that was a regular occurrence at 45 pounds.

Do you have any idea how wonderful it felt to slide into my seat without incident? And get up to use the restroom instead of painfully holding it in throughout the meal because I didn't want the embarrassment of asking the party next to me hoist their table away from mine to create enough space for my departure? It may sound like no big deal, but after being imprisoned by nearly 200 extra pounds, such freedom of movement is unmitigated glory.

Those of you hoping for a Sports Illustrated ending to my story, well, I think it's safe to say that, at age 49, the bikini ship has sailed. Maybe with some lipo, all my free time spent on cardio and sit-ups, and subsisting on egg white omelets (that's how the fitness models do it, I'm told), I'd have a shot, but I'm just not interested in that unreasonable a price tag.

I look good with my clothing on. I'm happy. I'm healthy. And I can take flights of stairs without sounding like a locomotive. All things I'd never thought would be a reality for me in this lifetime. Do you really think I'm going to spend an ounce of energy lamenting loose skin?

The Power of A Loving Touch

It was during the mid 90's when I was adrift, unhappy, 300 pounds, and searching for valid methods for getting unstuck that I was serendipitously connected with the philosophy of a woman named Carol Hansen Grey. The internet can be a wonderful thing, and in this particular instance, it put me in touch with someone who was reasonable, caring, and who had been there in terms of weight and self-loathing.

A former woman of size, Grey overcame a lifelong weight issue and the emotional fallout from divorce via a practice she invented that involved rubbing lotion all over her body in a very kind and deliberate fashion while saying aloud positive and affirming messages to her body. It may sound kooky. And it did to me at first…but only for a flash. On second thought, it sounded a heck of a lot better than the Cabbage Soup Diet, another bottle of miracle herbs, or me continuing on with the silent but toxic chorus of berating myself. So I gave it a shot. Every day – for months.

Dr. Rumki Banerjee, a medical doctor based in Glen Allen, Va., says that scientists have demonstrated time and again that physical illness is preceded by changes in an organism's electromagnetic field. And guess what influences the electromagnetic field? Emotions. And when I made that connection, I blanched, thinking of all the years of I silently and sometimes out loud sent a steady stream of criticism and insults to my body. And what had it gotten me? Certainly not looking or feeling better.

Hansen's positive reinforcement practice was a cassette tape of a lecture and instructions she gives on how to put the kindness in motion and the results she's experienced herself and seen in others' well being – very often weight loss. Despite practicing what Carol Hansen preached religiously, the weight did not come off as a result. For me, it was not an immediate result…I had years more time to put in at 300 pounds +, and considerabl more inner healing and other lessons to live through. There is no doubt, however, those words and the kind act of caressing myself not only planted seed, it healed me on a very important internal level. For anyone who doubts the truth of this, look up the documentary "The Hidden Messages in Water" on YouTube It clearly and scientifically illustrates how crucial it is to monito. and curate the words directed at self because they can either enhance your life force or diminish it.

The fact that I'm not banging the drum and singing promises

egularly practicing self-kindness will cause you to lose all your
nwanted weight and thereby dissolve all your pre-existing
roblems should have your attention. I'm not here to trick or
eceive, but rather, share what worked for me. It's a truth that
he diet industry wants you to turn away from. Dieting will not
ure what ails an emotional eater. Drugging oneself with food-
verload is a condition that is best treated with love, intelligence,
nd understanding...period.

xercising the Inalienable Right to Be Imperfect

here was something peculiar about Carla as she approached
ne from across the room. Her movement was unsteady and
he looked confused as she navigated the crowded room at
alling hours for a mutual friend who had passed away. When
Carla stepped closer to greet me she nearly lost her balance,
nd then, smell of alcohol-breath wafted invisibly between
s. Encountering someone so heavily intoxicated at a pubic
ereavement service was a first, so I braced myself. "You've done
 great job with the weight loss, Stacey, " she slurred. "But your
ss is really big... you've still got a fat ass." I stood in horrified
ilence with the friend I'd been conversing with. We were both
oo stunned to speak as Carla stumbled away, alcohol fumes
railing her departure like a caustic blast of dragon's breath.

Carla was hammered. But that didn't make her proclamation
o down any easier. I could feel the mercury of outrage rising
p in me. But I was there to comfort and support a grieving
amily who are dear friends of mine. It would not have been the
me to yank Carla by the throat to draw her perilously near to
ne so I could hiss through clenched teeth that she was being
happropriate. Instead, I took a deep breath, and let Carla make
er way around the room like a deranged bag lady.

My history with absorbing bigoted, vitriolic remarks about my size is long. Being a chubby child meant I was the object of much derisive amusement for the boys who rode my school bus, girls at summer camp, even babysitters. Even the safe haven of family reunions wasn't off limits. "Dear...come over here," one of my aunts said with a smile as she led me by the hand to a corner of the living room. "The next time you go to the beauty salon, ask the stylist if she'll part your hair on the side, because it'll make you look tall and skinny!" Not exactly the kind of attention an 11-year-old wants. The advice didn't catapult me into a different body type, and neither did diets, fad drinks, and exercise gadgets that promised to do the same. No surprise that I spent my formative years hating myself because I couldn't make myself change like everyone wanted. But I continued to jump into the saddle of diet after diet, and pored over women's magazines for guidance on how to be as alluring as I possibly could, even with the unfortunate hand I'd been dealt. I was exhausted by the grind and hadn't even hit my 20's.

More than half my life was spent bouncing between the extremes of dieting and binge-eating. For 20 years I weighed in excess of 300 pounds. I come from a long line of famine survivors, so my blood pressure and other stats were good, but my energy was non-existent. And I was tired of wearing black stretch leggings everyday.

Six years ago I embarked on a new way of living that had me dropping 180 pounds. I cut out gluten and cow dairy, but I also paid attention to the size of food portions and to the uncomfortable emotions that drove me to overeat in the first place. I started slow, but soon discovered I loved all forms of exercise, including yoga, distance-walking, and weight lifting.

Preceding the weight loss was the foundation of inner healing, or as I like to call it, reprogramming my mind. How could that not be part of the process with all the negative message that streamed in for so long? I also began to get irate and question the collective voice that said I wasn't OK simply because of the ize of my body. I still cherish the memory of me, at age 25, hasing down a "gang" of cowardly teenage boys at the mall vho mooed like cows in my direction and rocket-launched ames and from a safe distance. How satisfying it was when they cattered like rats as I, snorting mad, stormed over to confront hem.

love having 180 pounds off me and I'm very clear that being smaller size doesn't make me a better human being, it simply neans I'm freer. Still, I would have thought that the insults nd demeaning queries would have ended on that joyful day hat I was able to step into a size 8 pair of jeans. But as Carla so loquently proved, such a Utopian existence is not the case. It eems that even the formerly fat aren't exempt from our culture's voracious appetite for critiquing. Carla was hardly imparting new information to me. I'm fully aware (despite not having direct view of it) that my posterior is my largest and most pronounced... asset. And not so much in a Jennefer Lopez kind f way (I wish). Unlike JLo, my derriere is, well, not as tightly vound. I also know lipo-suction is an option. But it's an option haven't taken and I don't wish to explain or apologize for my hoice. Maybe it's too costly, or that I'm afraid of going under he knife, or the risks outweigh the benefits. Or maybe I'm imply exercising my right to be imperfect.

ven it if means having to field the occasional rude question, uch as "what's your goal weight?" or "have you gained weight?" es, someone really asked me that. Point blank. And it was a riend, whom I'll refer to as Martha. It's probably important to ote that Martha is obese. And it's also important to note that ny reaction was yet again stunned silence. Martha didn't just top at the question; she went on to announce that my arms idn't look as 'good' as they once did. And she was probably ight. I'd come out of a six-month injury to my shoulder that urtailed my lifting. OK, so I softened up, but should that green-ght scrutiny from others?

s Martha's question hung in the air, everything went kind of

2

blurry and I vaguely recall excusing myself from the room. It briefly flashed across my mind to lob back a 'who are you to talk?' retaliation, but I didn't want to play that game. It would be hypocritical and contrary to my deepest principles. Several weeks later she and I had a frank discussion about the incident via email. I accepted her apology and we've returned to good terms, but the dynamic between us has never been the same.

You did good, but not quite good enough is the message I've gotten from some who feel the need to assess the new me. So what to do with the Martha's and Carla's of the world? In Carla's case I chose not to resurrect the incident. It was highly unlikely that she'd remember it anyway. As for Martha, I know from my own character flaws that her disconnection to her obesity and the physical trap she's in prompted her to target someone else. Which is understandable, but no one's allowed to do that to me anymore.

Here's the truth that no woman should have to explain: I don't want to spend the majority of my time and energy pursuing an ideal that's not realistic for me. Knowing this is as freeing as having the weight off. It leaves me free to do things like write more books, spend time in the kitchen making food for people I love, do a challenging yoga workout, or even learn a new language.

I've done enough work on myself weight-wise. I'm happy with where I am. If you find that insufficient, that's you're problem. And if you come at me with an insulting remark about my proportions -- I'll be ready this time.

A 300-pound woman walks into the offices of Cosmopolitan magazine...

Oh...are you waiting for a punch-line? It wasn't the set-up to a joke. It's a scene from my life.

Picture it: New York City, March of 2000. There I am in the Hearst Building, which is to magazine publishing what the

Pentagon is to military defense. Clutching my reporter's notebook and a brand new pen, I stride into the marbled lobby, all 330 pounds of me. I'm coiffed, immaculately accessorized, dressed in city-chic all black, and I'm heading into the offices of Cosmopolitan magazine.

That's right. Cosmo. The home of wispy-thin cover models and pages of sage monthly tip-ridden features on 'how to make your hot sex life even hotter!' Deep stuff sells. And Cosmo is certainly proof of that. For anyone who doesn't know, Cosmopolitan is all about women aspiring to be FAB-U-LUUUS. And that starts with looking flawless.

Did I mention that my 37th-floor-destination was the inner lair of this shrine to female perfection? I was granted an interview with the magazine's editor-in-chief and I was both excited and a little buzzed with anticipation since I spent my 20's worshipping Cosmo covers and contents within. Yes, I was about 200 pounds over the acceptable weight limit by Cosmo-standards, but the other truth at play in this scenario is, after a lifetime of berating myself, I'd decided I'd had enough. So why not embrace the polaric opposite of wispy-thin and not simply accept myself, bu CELEBRATE who I am in all it's glory? I'm bigger than most women, so what? Is that a reason to cower in shame? For years I believed it was. Then one day I realized how ridiculous that was. I put the car of my mind-chatter in reverse and did a 180.

That sort of "Happy Chutzpah" is how I got the gig to interview Cosmo's editor-in-chief in the first place. As I stepped off the elevator, the first thing in my line of vision was a rack of clothin for a photo shoot, including a pair of minuscule capri pants that I probably couldn't have fit my arm into. But I remained undaunted as a polite receptionist accompanied me to Kate White's corner office for what turned out to be a voluptuous and very interesting interview…for both parties.

There's something about being looked at as handicapped or less than that makes one want, or perhaps need to try harder, do better, hit greater heights. I knew full well that the rules of the culture I lived in meant I was judged by my appearance. Lazy, less-than-competent, slovenly, and dull-minded were some of the misconceptions people put on me because of my largeness. So, (and this turned out to be a gift) I had to work a little harder than the average reporter. I did whatever it took to prove that a fat woman can be searingly insightful and intelligent. Also hard working, and quick on her feet.

"Stacey, I want to tell you something," Kate White said when our 3 hours was up and she walked me back to the elevator. "This is the best interview I've ever had. You asked great questions…. better than the reporters at the national morning show I was on last week." I stood there stunned, elated, and grateful. Ms. White was not only a gracious interview subject, she freely gave praise and credit when it was due. I thanked her profusely and as she waved goodbye, she made a promise to send off a note of praise to my boss. Kate White kept her word about the letter, but my boss (not the most nurturing knife in the drawer) ended up hiding it from me. And that's another show, Oprah, but my ensuing verbal scuffle with the less-than-encouraging boss was ust another glowingly-won battle in the war I waged to repair my self-esteem and stick up for myself in a world that said I wasn't worth a heck of a lot.

I share all this with you to make a point: The diet industry misses the mark in ways that are too many to enumerate. But one of them is this: manipulating calories and losing weight won't cause a life-changing breakthrough for most people. For emotional eaters and escape artists like myself, focusing on getting the weight off is putting the cart before the horse. It was a far more urgent matter for me to address the non-existent self-esteem and start buttressing it from the subterranean level on up. Ground zero happened to be at a weight that exceeded most NFL linebackers. So what? I didn't murder anyone, or steal money, or hurt someone's children. In my estimation, those are the three valid reasons for bearing shame. Weight just isn't in that category and it never should have been to begin with.

Some of you who have read my cookbook-memoir "Clean Comfort" know the denouement of my life story. I continue on as a 300-pound woman for nearly 20 years. One snowy day in January 2009, life gives me a series of wake-up calls. I'm ready to listen. And back up that listening with taking sane and measured action on the wake-up calls. In the process, I lose a whole lot of weight. I didn't just wake up one day and decided this should happen. It took years of focus, determination, and honoring myself in a world that said I had no right to be honored. These are the brass tacks of transformation. They have nothing to do with sweating at a gym or adhering to a particular food plan. Those are simply ancillary mechanics that aid with the calories in-calories out equation.

Solid change from within is takes for an emotional eater to spring herself from the hamster wheel. And that requires all those wonderful intangibles most weight loss gurus don't go near because, well, it simply isn't profitable for them. But that's the good news-bad news moral of the story. The answers are within you. And only you can decide that the time has finally come to believe in yourself.

Oh, and PS: it's going to feel really weird at first. Please don't let that deter you.

An Extremely Brief Dissertation on Loose Skin

Women are still trapped under a hyper-critical microscope,

sorry to say. The mail I get from readers sorrowfully reminds me that there is still work to be done. It's an inside job, ladies. Surgery, weight loss, and botox won't set you free. Only a loud and unapologetic declaration that you're OK with yourself will shove the microscope out of society's intrusive hand. Yes, even if you're not flawless, you're calling the game over. You've always been OK and now the world knows it. That became my mantra at 300 pounds and it's my mantra today. In part because the No. 1 concern I get from clients and readers of my books is from women fearing their happiness will be impaired by loose skin after a weight loss.

So, what do you do if you've dropped a lot of weight and have some loose skin? Off the top of my head, this comes to mind: GET OUT THERE AND LIVE YOUR FREAKIN' LIFE! I mean come on, life is a gift to begin with. And if you have a new lease on it because of releasing a substantial amount of weight, do you really think your primary focus will be on any residual imperfections? For me it wasn't even a distant concern. When you walk through life at 300 pounds + for 20 years, being free of that physical and emotional burden tends to elevate one into a tate of joy and gratitude…but maybe that's just me.

do understand the concern of loose skin. No one wants it, or
ctively seeks it out. But to be a slave to fearing or loathing it is
uying into our society's manic focus on looking flawless. It has
ecome a destructive fetish. All you have to do is Google 'plastic
urgery disasters' to see how easily the quest for 'looking good
nough' can spiral out of control. OK, love handles are lipo-
uctioned. I guess I look better…but what can I work on next?
h! a brow lift…followed by hair extensions and lip injections.
eah, that's the ticket! Then I'll be happy.

et me save you the thousands of dollars you may be poised to
pend (or borrow). If you're not in possession of some baseline
atisfaction with who you are…including how you look, surgery
on't magically wave that malady away. Surgery does nothing to
uiet or console the inner critic. That's your job.

nteresting point: All the loose-skin concerns I get from readers
re from women at the start of their journey. They'd actually
ve to get rid of the weight, but are wondering if loose skin is
o high a price to pay. Really? If that's going to roadblock you
efore you even start, it's likely you're not ready. I'm not judging,
ut let's call it like it is. Change can be unnerving; to you and
ose around you. I've lived it; I know. Just consider being
onest about what might really be holding you back. Never has
nyone who has dropped 100 pounds or more groused to me
ey don't like their skin. Why? They're simply too elated with
eir new life, which includes lots of freedom and energy. It's far
ore exhilarating than a perfection that doesn't exist.

I Weigh 50 Pounds More Than A Vogue Model ~ And I'm Ecstatic!

Oh, yoo-hooooo: Diet Industry, beauty magazines, Madison Avenue, I've got something to say to you.

I weigh 165 pounds.

That's it. No remorse necessary. I'm not ashamed, perturbed or disturbed in any way. Which is really good news for me, but not so great news for you. Oh, stop sniveling. Yeah, I know, you can't manipulate me anymore. But here's an idea. Maybe you could try and find a more honorable way of making a living.

Not only am I okay with my weight of, I'll say it again, 165 pounds. I'm ecstatic over it. I once weighed 345 pounds. Do you know how this must feel? Of course you don't. If you ever suffered the humiliation of being large in a fat-phobic society, or have known the abject frustration of failing at the maniacally devised human mouse traps and self-esteem crushers known as diets, you would be unable, in good conscience, to continue preying on the misery of others.

It may interest you to know I hoisted the 180-pound monkey off my back through clean eating, listening to my body's hunger cues, exercising regularly and deciding to go head to head with the demons that drove me to binge eat. Now that I'm free, I know that health and balance is a total mosaic. The number on the scale for me is no longer the ultimate indicator of this. I weigh above what many women, and certainly the modeling and entertainment industry deem acceptable. But I don't care anymore. I could choose to spend considerable energy on getting that number down another 20 or 30 pounds, but it eems I've reached a comfortable place and my body is happy. I xercise regularly, eat clean, and quite frankly, I'm not interested 1 being any more rigorous than I am. That's not to say I'll stop ccepting challenges, but enough's enough. It's okay to be happy rith myself, even if it in no way matches the media images we're ed ad infinitum.

know some of you have found peace, love and fitness through way of living that does not include gimmicks and legalized orture. Have you arrived at a place where you're happy with ourself, or are you constantly wringing your hands because you on't think you look good enough or weigh what you "should" veigh?

1y story does not have a Sports Illustrated ending to it. So rhat? Just because I'll never be whisked away to Bora Bora for tissue-with-straps-couture photo shoot doesn't mean my life bereft of happiness or meaning. My thighs are not smooth as eramic. The stretch marks were embedded at age 11, the bikini 1ip has sailed, and I know it. And somehow, I'm still walking pright, happier than I've ever been and grateful beyond leasure for my freedom.

Vho's with me in the victory charge? If enough of us rally, the d and diet industries will one day be forced to change their ocus, and perhaps they'll even become a little less shallow nd a lot more honorable with their intentions. A Recovering merican can dream, can't she?

Not Your Average Before Photo

Many of you may recognize this widely used 'before' shot of me at a 1996 wedding. It's pretty clear from the angle and the billowing dress that I weigh in excess of 300 pounds. Because of that inescapable fact and other less obvious reasons, the spark of my life force is unmistakably muted in this photograph. Carrying that amount of excess baggage in the physical sense siphoned an enormous amount of energy from me. And then there was the impetus for the physical baggage in the first place: I had stopped paying attention to who I really am, what I really want, how I really want to live.

Quite simply: I believed Happiness was out of my reach. And since it was meant for others and not me, I ate to dull the emptiness and dissatisfaction. But it still thundered within me. That's the thing about addiction; it doesn't really take care of the problem. But eating was the only tool I had at the time, and as you can see, I went with it.

On the surface, this photograph of me looking lifeless at age 30 in a prototypical Mother of The Bride dress seems like the cautionary tale that most 'before' photographs are. But this snapshot in time is far more than a warning. It's a tribute to the possibility of conquering odds. Swimming upstream against the majority is where my transformation really began. Not in

81

anuary 2009, when I began the process of releasing weight.

his upstream voyage was a crucial part of my learning on the
ath I walked of pain, so-called failures, and even Joy. Believe it
r not, there was Joy involved for me at the wedding reception
f my friend Bill and his new bride, Tracy. I may not have
ved where I was physically, but I was in the middle of a very
nportant life lesson and without it, I wouldn't be writing this
log entry today at half my size.

was speeding full-throttle into the unknown territory of loving
yself no mater what the scale said. Anyone who's ever spent
ven a little time in the United States knows what a radical and
ourageous and outrageous move this was on my part. Look
t me. By every standard measured against me by the society I
as raised in, I should have been at home with the blinds down
a a fetal position. Believe me, for a long time, I bought into the
elusion that people of size aren't quite fully human.

here was no major moment of epiphany…just gradual
acrements of awakening to the Truth. And when I began to see
nd more importantly, feel the Truth about the unchangeable
ature of my worth, it became easier and easier to question the
nessages from outside 'authorities.' I began getting more and
nore comfortable with something: A flicker of hope at my core
nat would not die. Lit from a mysterious source, an unknown
lace, it remained intact, even after all the years spent trying to
ill it. It emanated this clear message: 'I Deserve.'

was far from being in a state of happiness and balance, but I
as on my way. That's the magic message I want to give you
day. Start right where you are - I did.

Vhat this photograph doesn't reveal is the rest of what unfolded
a that ballroom of the Saratoga Springs Holiday Inn: The DJ
t one of my favorite and most life-affirming disco songs of all
me rip. The pulsating beat of Cheryl Lynn's "Got to Be Real"
alled me as I sat there, safely anchored in my chair. It called me

again as I hesitated. I didn't love how I looked. I was way bigger than anyone in the room. How would me up there on the dance floor look? What would they think? And then I realized that getting out there and being in those few moments of joy while this amazing song played mattered more than the doubts. So I got up and danced...in front of everyone.

I didn't wait for the magic moment of looking a certain way. My transformation had already taken root and it got a major growth spurt that day on the dance floor as I took my place under the glitter ball and agreed to get real, arms open wide to whatever lay ahead.

Divesting from the Messiah Myth

Do you have a Messiah Complex? Don't be hard on yourself if you do: it's a common side-effect of a culture that encourages us to seek solutions in miracle-inducing products and gadgets. As a retired dieter, I've certainly had my share of placing all my precious eggs in the basket of my latest savior-du-jour. It's part of the human make-up because it's so tempting, the idea of a magic wand to eradicate what ails us. I'm not knocking anyone's belief system, but Sigmund Freud was onto something when he posited that many of us are looking for a 'Cosmic Daddy' to take care of things for us. Just take a look at the self-help aisle of the bookstore. And any insomniac can tell you that the TV airwaves before and after Prime Time are saturated with infomercials, many of them shameless in their dangling of promises for cellulite free thighs or a face so tight and beautiful, you just may end up with a modeling contract.

Nowhere have I seen my own Messiah Complex manifest more noticeably than in the merry-go-round cycle of dieting, falling off the wagon, climbing on the wagon, and scolding myself unmercifully...anyone know what I'm talking about?

My recent attempt at a messianic solution started as it often does, with trance-like gravitation towards the home shopping channels. Flipping to a network so devoted to and adept at slick sales pitches delivered at the tail end of December is probably one of the most dangerous things someone with an unrequited Messiah Complex can do. The profit-hungry networks are known for being as brilliant as they are ruthless when it comes to marketing the "it's gonna be a whole new you!" variety of glittery hope after weeks of holiday gluttony.

It was late December '08 when, bloated, overstuffed with Christmas cookies, and at weighing in at 345 pounds, I was more than a little vulnerable to transformation promises. To say I ached with discouragement would have been an understatement. Therefore, I was ripe for the picking as I watched in wide-eyed wonder an uber-thin actress who's never had a heavy day in her life, chirping an endorsement for an exercise sort of contraption that looked like little more than a metal folding chair with a few pullys. You'd think the act that the actress was, during her decades-long career in front of the camera all of 105 pounds soaking wet would have been a tip-off where the transformative powers of the chair she was hawking was concerned. But when you're desperately seeking a Messiah, logic has left the building. All I could see was the promise of what I would look like if I simply placed the order. (Did I mention that when one is frothing after a Messiah figure, there's a tendency to become delusional?) It only took about 8 minutes of convincing this gloriously photogenic creature, her luxurious mane of hair bouncing elegantly off her petite shoulders as she deftly mounted the contraption and began waving a leg in the air behind her. And what did it matter that I was over the weight limit, per the manufacturer's warning? I needed saving and this was the invention that would rescue me. My rationale was that being over the weight limit would be the perfect incentive to get myself motivated and into high gear.

Somewhere in between placing the $300 order and the surfboard-sized package arriving at my door a week later, I realized the error of my snap-decision and sent it back unopened. That's the advantage of years of false starts. They had both worn me down and also gilded me with the wisdom of experience. I knew before even taking a box cutter to the cardboard that my misguided order had false-start written all over. It was time to put my wake-up call into action and return the snake oil to sender.

Fortunately, only days later, my true epiphany came: seeing a radiant Carnie Wilson on Oprah January 5. A quick Google search of 'Carnie and Dallas' brought me to a philosophy known as DDPYOGA, and somewhere between bending back into a Diamond Cutter and grunting out a Broken Table I realized that no Messiah was necessary (at least in terms of exercise equipment). We ARE the Messiah. The workout program that Diamond Dallas Page designed works the anatomy better than any machine. Since body and soul are intertwined, the workout not only strengthened my physicality, they bolstered my confidence, vitality, and overall connection with life.

DDP has always said that you'll get out of it what we put into it, and from the start, that admonition was a glorious departure from the Messiah Complex: there was no looking to anyone or anything else but me for results. No one's going to save me but me…and no Thighmaster, Total Gym, or squeaky Pilates chair is going to lift me out of my life on a magic carpet ride to health and happiness. Whatever those machines can do for my muscles I can do for myself with moves that involve me, some serious effort, and simple gravity. That's it. No gadgetry needed. And what, you might be asking, has exercise to do with the soul Quite a bit, as I've learned in the past decade. What comprises us is all interwoven: tending to the body irrevocably tends the soul and visa versa. Quite simply, the care and strengthening of the body has a direct effect on the quality of our life-force-energy and our inner-selves.

Anyone who doubts me has never done a Broken Table…or

etter yet, Broken Airplane. Depending on the DDPYOGA
nove, the strength and physical discipline needed to achieve
·roper execution can be subtle or overwhelming. Yeah, there's
vork involved. But it's work that I'm doing. This is my body and
ıy life…I don't want some machine stepping in and trying to
ıke my place.

How Did Transformation Begin?
By Accepting All 300 Pounds of Me

he boarding pass in my hand was damp and crumpled, a result
f me clutching it a little too tightly as I waited to board a plane
ɔ Nashville for my maiden voyage as a freelance travel writer.
d recently departed the safety a 9-to-5 job because I wanted
ıore freedom. Now that I had it, I was terrified. It wasn't flying I
:ared, but the dreaded task of squeezing my 330-pound body
ıto an airline seat and possibly perturbing the traveler seated
eside me. The flight was predictably uncomfortable. I sat for
ıost of the journey with hips twisted at an angle to conform to
ıe parameters of the narrow seats in coach. I was most grateful
ɔr the kind-hearted gentleman seated to the left of my aisle seat.

If he minded that I
spilled past his
armrest, he didn't
let it show. It was
December 2006,
and I was making
good on my vow to
not let my weight
stop me from living
life. Looking back,
I'm in awe of my

ravery, because life at 300 pounds wasn't easy.

lifetime of dieting and regaining weight prompted my live-your-life-anyway vow. As a child, I was mildly chubby but was teased for it anyway. I soon found myself using food as a comfort and escape. At home, safely away from the Greek chorus of insults, I ate out of shame and unexpressed rage. Using food to soothe a throbbing emotion was a survival skill I acquired before I reached double digits in age. Because it was a skill interwoven with relief and enjoyment, it was easy to cultivate, and by age 10, I weighed 120 pounds. That revelation was followed by a visit to a doctor who prescribed for me a crash diet consisting mostly of stewed vegetables and broiled protein. I felt my heart sink as he slid the typewritten list of permissible foods across his desk. It was a short and sterile itemization, and nowhere on it did I see butter. Ten days later, and much to my parents' disappointment, I could take no more and retreated to the comfort zone of scrambled eggs with buttered toast.

It was the beginning of an on-again, off-again cycle of dieting and overeating that repeated throughout my school years. At age 17, I left the pain of school behind for good in a billowing yellow graduation gown and a weight of 230 pounds. During my 20s, there were two 100-pound weight losses induced by a toxic combination of white-knuckle willpower and self-loathing. Both times, I regained the weight, plus more. Looking back, my cardinal mistake was in buying society's hype that happiness equaled being thin. I had only fixed the "problem" externally. The excess weight was gone, but inside I still felt like the inadequate fat girl. By age 30 I tipped the scales at 306 pounds. I was both horrified and worn out by the revelation. So what was a hardcore overeater to do? I gave up, took myself out of the race and decided I'd have more overall peace if I simply accepted myself. Not only had I reached my limit with dieting, any tolerance I harbored for size bigotry was evaporated by years of snide remarks and degrading comments. I began to question the entire equation and decided I deserved respect no matter what I looked like, no matter what the scale said.

On that voyage to Nashville a new and vibrant culture with visits to the Grand Ole Opry, Country Music Hall of Fame, botanical

ardens, historic homes, and all the soul food I could get my
ands on. Travel and discovery were exhilarating and fun...
nd I'd been waiting my entire life to experience them. Other
ravel assignments had me splashing on beaches in Puerto Rico,
lathering myself in mud at the Dead Sea in Israel, solemnly
ouring the Anne Frank House in Amsterdam, and preparing
rench food at a cooking school in Wisconsin. At a pricey West
Coast destination spa, I proudly took my place in line at Zumba
lass and shimmied side by side with picture-perfect housewives
lus a celebrity or two.

he adventures were fulfilling, but the truth was, my weight was
 burden. Walking, carrying luggage, taking stairs, climbing in
nd out of tour vans, and seating myself at restaurant banquettes
vere all more difficult thanks to schlepping nearly 200 extra
ounds on my 5-foot-8-inch frame.
was tired and listless much of the time, but I carried on this
vay another three years, until life delivered an unexpected
vake-up call on Jan. 5, 2009 with both the revelation that my
veight was at a high of 345 pounds and learning there was a
ormer pro wrestler out there who was helping out-of-shape
eople reclaim their lives and health. Viewing the YouTube
ransformation of his most famous success story, a formerly
bese and injured Gulf War veteran, Arthur Boorman, was all
ie information I needed.

It's truly amazing how
powerful that intangible
thing known as hope is...
Seeing Arthur Boorman
walk again after being on
canes for 15 years signaled
that I too could rehabilitate
my body – if I was willing to
work hard for it.

Vhat I wasn't willing to do were any of the old tricks that got me
i the obesity hole in the first place. I wanted to cement habits I

could live with and even enjoy. This new philosophy could in no way resemble a diet. So I began cooking meals at home rather than living on fast food and inventory from the chips aisle. After 20 years of wearing black spandex leggings and trapeze tops, I was ready to take direction and combine it with my own wisdom. I ate when I was hungry and stopped when satisfied. I built my strength by doing DDPYOGA regularly, and later that year, I walked a marathon in New York City.

My transformation also required an honest look at what drove me to overeat. For many years, three main life situations contributed to my misuse of food: a stressful office job, an unhappy relationship, and deep sadness over the process of losing my father to Alzheimer's disease. I didn't deal with all three at once; that would have been overwhelming. But I decided it was time to wake up and face them. I remedied the job situation by quitting it to pursue my passion. My boyfriend at the time was not a bad guy at all, but it was a relationship of safety and convenience for both of us. We knew it deep down but never touched the truth in terms of discussion. I chose to hide this way for decades, overeating to compensate for the emptiness I felt. In 2009, I finally found the courage to be truthful with him, and we parted as friends.

The last hurdle was the most painful: witnessing my father's decline, and what a long process it was. He lay in a nursing home bed for nearly a decade, nonverbal and unaware of the world around him, and my heart ached every time I visited his room at the nursing room, it never got easier. For the first half of his illness, I ate myself into oblivion. For the latter, I stood squarely in reality and waded through the feelings. I was there for my father and for myself like never before. And when his time finally came, I was able to embrace it and be there at his side, fully present with my tears, my sorrow, my gratitude.

I'm revealing all this to show what's involved in lasting transformation. The diet industry wants to keep people like me trapped. I'm just another average hardcore overeater who made out of the woods. I'm living proof that it's possible. Especially since I was 44 when I began -- the time in a woman's life when metabolism is alleged to grind to a halt and from which life is said to go steadily downhill. Now in my 50s, I look and feel better than I did in my 20s. I love being a smaller size, but I'm clear that it doesn't make me a better person. I suffered too much with size bigotry to play that game. What it does make me is free.

I no longer panic when boarding a plane and I love shopping for clothing. I wear any color I want and no longer have to settle for what fits. For 20 years it was black, head to toe, even during sweltering summer months. Heat waves, airplane seats, and delicate folding chairs no longer bring me to my knees. I'm also in a relationship with one of the kindest, most romantic guys on the planet. Yes, it seems life has decided I'm to be compensated for the years of social isolation, and invitations to the prom never extended. I must say, the spontaneous bouquets of flowers and candle-lit dinners were worth the wait, and are sweeter and more appreciated in middle age. Bill is also a fabulous cook and trusted healthy-recipe developer for the three cookbooks we wrote together. Bill loves me for who I am and embraces who I once was. And there's no way I could have been in a position to receive all the wonderful good stuff into my life if my self-esteem hadn't been repaired and restored to its rightful solid foundation. Inner-transformation always precedes the outer. Without exception.

Put Your Hands in the Air Where I Can See 'Em and Drop the Denial

The human mind is a brilliant and complex system of wiring and synapses, all designed for specific functions such as memory, deductive thinking, reflexes, and oh yes, protection.

We all come equipped with this little entity that's highly effective in shielding us from things we'd rather not focus on. The spectrum of things the mind would prefer to avoid runs from unpleasantness to trauma – Denial works at masking it all. And sometimes, that's a good thing. Reliving the unbearable details of a traumatic experience are often too much to deal with – ever – and the mind sees to it that certain memories in our vault appropriately never see the light of day.

Then there are irritants far less impactful in their severity, but troublesome nonetheless: pretending to be happy in a marriage or a chosen profession when you're really not, turning a blind eye from a freeloading adult child, or being blissfully unaware of a steadily increasing weight gain. The latter situation is how I lived for most of my adult life. I essentially told my psyche I didn't want to see or hear any truth about my growing size. To deal with my expanding hips and belly, I simply wore black most of the time and made sure all garments were made of stretchy lycra. Denim? Who needs it? And I don't like the color blue anyway. Someone wants to take my picture? Not if I can help it! And then I would proceed to evacuate the premises like, well, like my denial depended on it.

After decades of eating rebelliously, a moment of reckoning came in 2009 when I stepped on the doctor's scale and it registered 345 pounds. I had no idea how it was to happen, but he time had come to turn the ship around. All I knew at the time was, I did not want to continue down the road I was raveling and have the numbers one day reach 400. I prayed for guidance and protection from snake oil masquerading as weight-loss solutions. What came my way was a no-nonsense fitness guru named Diamond Dallas Page. He was a former pro wrestler who had a second career rehabilitating out-of-shape Americans. Based on the photos of him from his website, DDP looked a bit irate and probably not in possession of a lot of patience. My inner quest through the world of spirituality and self-help had given me plenty of mentors who were the gentle, hand-holding types, and that was exactly what I needed at the time. But for this particular leg of my journey, I needed an attitude of unbending steel. I can still hear DDP's voice growling at me through the phone lines on one of our cross-country conversations. "TAKE the photos," he ordered, after I protested getting 'before' shots of my 345-pound frame the fifth time. He was adamant about me having a cache of before photos to look back on. "Don't worry," I shot back. "I'll know when I'm losing weight…heck, I'll keep all my old wardrobe so I'll be able to measure the difference." A valiant try on my part, but Diamond Dallas Page was having none of it.

"TAKE the pictures. It's something you NEED to do."

What a hard-ass, I muttered, moments after the conversation came to an end with a 'that's final' sendoff from DDP. Why is it so crucial…why? My heart was raging like a caged animal. Truth was closing in on me. It was a tenacious dread I felt inside of me that reminded me of being eight years old and sitting, rigid with fear, in the examining chair of my ear doctor. I knew he'd be poking around my infected, throbbing ear and that it would hurt…but in the long run, there'd be healing.

Even before I asked a close friend to photograph me from all angles, my heart knew why DDP insisted I take this step; it was an unavoidable bridge to cross if I was to move forward. The minute I gazed at the photos I felt my throat tighten and braced myself for the tidal wave. Suddenly I was sobbing and had to look away from the woman I didn't recognize. The denial I had put so carefully in place to cushion me from reality had just been stripped away. As it turned out, the thief in the night was something denial couldn't toy with: a photograph. No wonder I refused getting my picture taken for the past 20 years. Through my mind's biased lens, whenever I gazed into the mirror, I didn't have a double chin, or a pudgy face, rotund stomach or 71-inch hips. But the camera spares no truthful detail and there it all was for me to digest. It was almost too much to bear...not so much my size and appearance, but the fact that I had gotten so adept, so chillingly excellent, at lying to myself. I had always prided myself on being an honest person. In general, I lived by the Golden Rule and didn't lie to others or deceive them. But when it came to my relationship with me, I tossed my morals out the window, commenced weaving the tall tales, and didn't even realize I was doing it.

Looking back at the incident through the lens of time, I'm now able to see that DDP knew what he was doing: he didn't just want a collection of photos for before and after purposes – he wanted me to take an accurate look at myself because I couldn't proceed to get real unless I did. How could I have ascertained a viable plan of action if I didn't taken an accurate look at how far down the canyon of destruction and denial I had fallen?

I'm grateful beyond words for this breakthrough. It was years in the making and took someone with the bedside manner of a marine sergeant to push me into action. Left to my own devices I would not have ventured into the bright, unrelenting light of reality. Sure, my breakthrough caused a significant amount of emotional upheaval, and it was all a necessary part of the healing process. For nearly three days, I cried off and on. With

he gates flung open at last, the deluge of emotions ranged from
orrow to disgust to anger. Fortunately, Terri Lange, the other
alf of my mentoring team was there to provide the calming yin
ɔ DDP's pile-driving yang.

Stacey, stop beating yourself up this instant!" she admonished
ia e-mail after I confessed how appalled I was at the mess I
1ade. Self-esteem at any size is a valid concept and always will
e as far as I'm concerned. On the other hand, however, I had
eliberately looked away at the downside of all my excess weight
nd its energetic, physical, and spiritual burden. From this I've
ome to learn that two truths can simultaneously exist: the
alidity of my worth as a human being is neither enhanced or
iminished by the numbers on the scale. AND too much excess
ʳeight on my body is, for me, an undesirable situation.

allowed myself the space and unhurried pace of processing
ʳhat spontaneously combusted on my emotional spectrum at
ny given moment in the days that followed. The truth began
ɔ feel increasingly non-threatening. Eventually, I was able to
ather the fractured parts of me shattered by the long-overdue
last of reality. I patiently began to shift out of scolding and
emorse to empathy and objectivity where the photos were
oncerned. They were a representation of what I looked like, not
ʳho I was. I am greater than my appearance and always will be.

hose 'before' photos taken in my living room that winter day in
009 had no bearing on my worth, but I was left with no choice
ut to admit they were a reflection of how I chose to handle life's
hallenges in an unhealthy way. Eventually, I had the courage to
ost the photos online. As time went on it got easier to be more
ɔrthcoming with myself. I forgive myself for the lies and self-
eceit; they were worn-out defense mechanisms and I'm grateful
ɔ say that a decade later, they feel as foreign to me as ordering
alf a drive-thru menu to take the edge off a bad day.

I Don't Need to Be Forgiven

Hold on to your love handles... because I'm about to present a transformation story with a heaping cup of uncustomary truth. The photo below might frighten you a little bit, but the truth is, you should never be afraid of the truth! This is how I look at the middle age of 51, post-180-pound-weight loss, and without the benefit of skin tightening surgery. I brought this change about through clean eating, regular movement, and paying attention to who I am. The latter is an ongoing process that involves riding out bad moods and dark days without downing enough chip-aisle-offerings for a family of six.

I understand if the accompanying photo is off-putting...I mean, I 100% get it. How could it not be jarring? The standard images we get of women post-weight-transformation are almost always in a sleeveless mini-dress of some sort or a bikini. It's become as standard as it is deceitful and insulting. Because it subtly implies that this is how we're supposed to look after months of disciplin and arduous work on oneself.

People who knew me at my former size often don't recognize me if we haven't seen each other in a while. Relative newcomers to my life are astonished at the before pictures. And then there's th segment of America whom I have let down, for I have not arrived at my destination in a bikini. It's true... when was in the highly-focused weight loss phase of my life, which lasted about tw years, I deliberately abstained from the steady rounds of Kool-Aid being serve to women like me. The refrain is as common as it is antiquated, but it's still sadly a part of our culture, this bikini fetish. Most weight transformation stories spotlighted in national forums such as "The Today Show" and "Shape"

magazine aren't complete without this syrupy, yawningly-predictable finale. It's about as heart-stirring as inspection by a code-enforcer, because that's essentially what it is.

Here's the deal American media: An itsy bitsy bikini was never on my radar. How could it have been? I've dealt with excess weight since childhood. The stretch marks were embedded at age 11. I weighed above 300 pounds for 20 years and didn't begin releasing weight in earnest until the age of 44. Now you see why the two-piece ship has sailed…and I'm OK with it. The standard 'after shot' is something I could probably achieve if I were to get significant amounts of cosmetic surgery while simultaneously emulating the eating habits of a fitness model, and I'm just not a fan of egg white omelets.

I've made all the sacrifices I'm willing to make. There's food I'd love to still be eating, but it's now off the list, in part because it's an emotional trigger and also because the nutritional content is sub-par. Exercise is a regular part of my life, but not in a militaristic sense. I face uncomfortable feelings and confront unpleasant people and situations rather than run from them. Why does this work in my favor? Because it's a formula I can live with. Channeling more of my time and energy to reach a more stringent (and kind of meaningless) goal is where I draw the line. Think about it: this is a brilliant way to practice boundary-setting….and a declaration of boundaries is something that's crucial to my wellbeing.

So, loose skin, fat pockets and all, I have no apologies to offer. Why should I? I was a worthy human being before the weight loss. Now I'm simply that same worthy person who's lighter and freer. I simply don't waste precious energy wringing my hands that I don't look like Gigi Hadid. In the interest of full disclosure, I wouldn't MIND looking like her, but that's not the hand life dealt me. Instead, I feel it's far wiser to focus on all the good in my life, including just how miraculous and wonderful my body is and how good it has been to me. And my amazing body continues to shower me with strength, vitality, good health, and other blessings. At this stage of the game, complaining about minutiae isn't on my radar. I have only room for thankfulness. Which isn't such great news to trend purveyors like Dr. Oz. Why, it's almost as if there might be a silent conspiracy to make women perpetually dissatisfied with themselves….'ya THINK?

So take a good look at this transformation story with the unconventional outcome. I'm very happy with it. This IS the equivalent of my bikini shot. It's where I've landed after years of self-hatred and turmoil. Not good news to the diet and beauty industries, but more and more of us are becoming de-programmed enough to rely on gut-checks rather than the offensive string-pulling of big business...and that is where the root of all transformation begins.

89783927R00057

Made in the USA
Middletown, DE
19 September 2018